What You'll Discover Inside This Book

Wheel:Life publications center on sharing resources ~~~~~~~~~~ who use wheelchairs. In this book, you'll discover a state-by-state directory of accessible travel destinations across the United States.

These accessible travel suggestions are part of the Get Out & Enjoy Life program that is a joint educational initiative between Wheel:Life, a global community of wheelchair users, and SPORTS 'N SPOKES magazine, published by the Paralyzed Veterans of America.

Why does this book cost $1.99?
Simple. We are relying on the sale of this resource to help fund other Wheel:Life programs that benefit the wheelchair community we serve. However, if money is an issue – please send us a note at http://wheel-life.org/contact-us/ and we will gladly forward a free .PDF copy to you.

For less than two dollars, you'll find that each chapter of this book provides easily-accessible destinations that are fun and engaging for friends who use wheelchairs.

Discovering is an easy, encouraging read that will help you explore all kinds of travel destinations, whether you are new to using a wheelchair or a seasoned pro.

So what are you waiting for? The first step to discovering new destinations with friends and family is to get started on Chapter 1.

Table of Contents

Foreword: Thank You to Our Readers and Sponsors	3
Get Out & Enjoy Life	10
Alabama	11
Alaska	14
Arizona	16
California	18
Colorado	23
Delaware	25
Florida	27
Georgia	29
Hawaii	32
Idaho	34
Illinois	36
Indiana	39
Iowa	41
Kentucky	44
Maryland	45
Massachusetts	47
Michigan	49
Minnesota	51
Mississippi	53
Missouri	54
Nevada	56
New Jersey	58
New York	60
Ohio	63
Oklahoma	65
Oregon	67
Pennsylvania	69
Rhode Island	72
South Carolina	73
Tennessee	75
Texas	77
Utah	80
Vermont	81
Virginia	82
Washington	83
Washington, DC	87
Wisconsin	89
Wyoming	90
Additional Travel Sources	92
National Parks and Golden Access Pass	96
Share Your Own Story of Discovering	97
Dedication	98
Wheel:Life Book Series	99

Foreword: Thank You to Our Readers and Sponsors

You may wonder how Wheel:Life is able to run a community website, offer free motivational giveaways, run several social media pages and publish books like this for you to use as an educational resource? Well, we couldn't do it alone, that's for sure.

First, we wouldn't have a reason to keep plugging away every day if it wasn't for our readers. Thank you for being one of them! We hope that you'll find value in Wheel:Life resources and that they will help you in your daily life.

If you would like to stay connected with Wheel:Life and receive updates on a regular basis when we publish new resources and articles on our main website, send us a note at: http://wheel-life.org/contact-us/ and we'll add you to our free monthly e-newsletter list.

Or, feel free to follow us on social media at:
- Facebook – https://www.facebook.com/wheellifeonline
- Twitter – www.twitter.com/wheellifeonline

Second, a group of fantastic organizations have come together to sponsor the Wheel:Life community. They are helping to fund all of the resources that you'll find on our main website [http://www.wheel-life.org] as well as those on our connected social media pages.

Thank you to all of the sponsors below for joining Wheel:Life in our effort to support people who use wheelchairs, worldwide. **To become a Wheel:Life sponsor, please contact us for details at: http://wheel-life.org/contact-us/**

Abilities Expo

Now in six cities across the nation, each **Abilities Expo** offers three days of access to the latest technologies and resources for ALL disabilities, informative workshops on issues that most resonate with the Community and fun activities like adaptive sports, dance, assistive animal demos and more. Come to the Expo! Get your free pass at www.abilitiesexpo.com.

BARD | CARE
Care. Comfort. Choice

For over 100 years, Bard Medical Division has been developing manufacturing and marketing disposable medical devices and catheters for urological and continence care applications.

The all silicone MAGIC3® Intermittent catheter line is the latest example of our commitment to providing innovative solutions to address the needs of consumers, caregivers and clinicians. It is a hydrophilic catheter that offers a touch-free insertion sleeve for easier handling and an exclusive 3 layer design for comfortable, easy and reliable catheterization. The all-silicone construction is soft and designed to be gentle on delicate urethral tissue.

For more information or instructions on obtaining a sample, call 800.243.3315 or visit www.BardMedical.com.

BLVD.com

BLVD.com is the nation's top choice for finding Wheelchair Vans For Sale. A complete selection of New, Used and Pre-Owned wheelchair vans for sale from top rated wheelchair van dealers nation-wide. You can also search a large selection of private party wheelchair vehicles for sale. Whether you're a disabled driver or passenger, we're here to help you find the right mobility equipment or vehicle modifications to fit your needs. Be sure to check our Wheelchair Vans page for resources on available wheelchair vehicle conversions, you can also apply for a wheelchair van loan in just minutes. Blvd.com is here to help you regain your freedom again! Learn more at: http://www.blvd.com or call 877-833-2480.

COLOURS

Colours Wheelchairs has become a turning point in the disability market since 1992 when Colours introduced our first active rigid wheelchair weighing a mere 16 lbs. Since then, we have been responsible for many great products including a four wheel independent suspension wheelchair (BOING!®) and another record lightweight wheelchair (ZEPHYR®) weighing 14.5 lbs. Yes, we believe we produce some of the best wheelchairs in the world. But, that is not what we are bragging about. What we are really proud of are the people who are using our chairs. They are, in our eyes, individuals who have a spirit unmatched by our competition. So, our thanks go to you, the customer, for joining the Colours Family and doing what you do best! www.colourswheelchair.com

Comfort Medical®

Based in Coral Springs, FL, Comfort Medical, LLC is the leading national mail-order provider of urological and ostomy supplies. Comfort is committed to supporting the needs of patients and healthcare professionals by providing a diverse product offering, convenient home delivery, education and support. Comfort Medical, LLC is a wholly-owned subsidiary of Liberty Medical Holdings, LLC. Learn more at http://www.comfortmedical.com or call 1-800-700-4246.

CURE

The Cure Commitment is unsurpassed in the industry. Only Cure Medical has committed to donating 10% of net income to scientific research for spinal cord injury. Only Cure Medical catheters are DEHP and BPA free. Simply by using new Cure Catheters® or Cure Catheter® Closed Systems for routine intermittent catheterization, you take part in the sustained pursuit of a cure. Learn more at www.curemedical.com.

EZ-ACCESS®
Breaking Through Barriers™

Family-owned and operated for 30 years, EZ-ACCESS is the leader in accessibility. We are dedicated to providing the highest quality, dependable and durable products to help you live your life to the fullest. Driven by our commitment to enrich lives by providing access to life beyond barriers, EZ-ACCESS®, a division of Homecare Products Inc., was founded in 1984 by Glenda Everard and her daughter, Deanne Sandvold. In 1988, son Don Everard joined the family business, bringing with him marketing expertise. This trio was the driving force behind the expansion of the ramp market, having pioneered the industry through the marketing and manufacturing of EZ-ACCESS portable wheelchair ramps.

EZ-ACCESS operates out of two locations. Headquarters and West Coast manufacturing are located in Algona, Washington, 15 miles south of Seattle and East Coast manufacturing is located in Morganfield, Kentucky, where the company reinforces its family-based philosophy with customers, employees and community alike. The two manufacturing facilities enable faster and less expensive deliveries across the nation to all their customers. Learn more at www.ezaccess.com

GRIT

The GRIT Freedom Chair is the most versatile chair on the market, designed from the ground up to handle any terrain. From trails to grass to snow, the Freedom Chair is built for you to push yourself. Born out of research at MIT, the Freedom Chair's patented easy-push levers reduce shoulder strain and put you in control of your mobility. Moving parts are composed of standard bicycle parts, so it's easy to customize or repair at your local bike shop. Ready to hit the trails? Learn more about the GRIT Freedom Chair at www.gogrit.us.

Hollister

Hollister Incorporated is an independently-owned global company that develops, manufactures, and markets healthcare products, servicing over 90 countries. From the earliest days of our company, there has been a strong sense of community – a connection to people. That connection is embedded in the very fabric of our company, and as we continue to develop new products and services, we are focused on meeting the healthcare needs of people throughout the global community.

Hollister Continence Care helps give the gift of independence to people whose lives have been affected by spinal cord injury by developing exceptional research-driven urological products and services. We are committed to people and to helping empower their lives. Everything we do is informed by a single guiding principle: People First. Our products and services are testimony – first and foremost – to the assurance that quality of life needn't be compromised by managing one's continence. Learn more at www.hollister.com.

Ki Mobility
Better by Design

Doug Munsey and Murray Slagerman founded Ki Mobility in 2005. With a combined experience of over 50 years in the complex rehab industry it is their comprehensive knowledge that drives Ki Mobility to achieve the success we share today.

We started small, in size and scope, determined to design a high quality lightweight folding wheelchair that responds like a rigid. The Catalyst lines innovative design concepts breathed new life back into the folding wheelchair market. Three additional product lines in the pediatric, rigid and tilt-in-space categories have since launched with similar success.

Although we have experienced steady growth through the years, the high level of personalized service and a keen attention to detail remains. With an emphasis on remembering what is important and what it is that makes a difference in the industry we continue to move forward. Visit www.kimobility.com.

LoveYourNurse provides free online CE for nurses through our partners' websites. Because nurses do so much for so many and ask for nothing in return, our mission is to provide access to free quality continuing education for hard working nurses. If your organization relies on nurses to keep you going, then show them some love. Register at LoveYourNurse.com and you give them all the Continuing Education they need. We promise they'll love you for it. http://www.loveyournurse.com

melio™

The innovative, new **Melio Self-Emptying Leg Bag System** gives catheter users a new level of independence, control, and dignity. It's the leg bag that empties at the touch of a button – and tells you when it's time. Made by Albert Medical Devices, an award-winning medical technology company located in the United Kingdom, Melio was created by founder Trevor Wills after his father experienced a severe stroke which required him to use a a urinary catheter and urine collection bag. Since its original development, the Melio Self-Emptying Leg Bag System has transformed the lives of catheter users on both sides of the Atlantic. Learn more at **www.meliolegbag.com**.

Mobility Management is the only industry publication written especially for mobility and rehab suppliers and clinicians. Mobility dealers/providers and rehab professionals turn to Mobility Management every month for real-world solutions regarding new Medicare/Medicaid policies, client assessment, product innovations, pending legislation, auto and home accessibility and end-user views. Learn more at: http://mobilitymgmt.com.

SPORTS 'N SPOKES is a bimonthly publication produced by the Paralyzed Veterans of America. S'NS reports on competitive sports and recreation for wheelchair users. Since 1975, S'NS has been a leader in wheelchair sports coverage and currently goes to more than 43 countries worldwide. Our readers come from all walks of life all having one thing in common: determination! SPORTS 'N SPOKES is committed to providing a voice for the wheelchair sporting and recreation community. Visit **www.sportsnspokes.com** to view the latest issue.

SPECIAL OFFER FOR OUR READERS

Since 1975, SPORTS 'N SPOKES has been the premier magazine for wheelchair sports and recreation.

SPORTS 'N SPOKES magazine is published by the Paralyzed Veterans of America and is the leading magazine for wheelchair sport enthusiasts with a readership spanning 40 countries.

New magazine subscribers will receive a one-year subscription for a discounted rate of $18.
One Year/Six Issues - (U.S. Only)

Just use promotion code **SNSFB** when ordering to receive your discount.

To contact SPORTS 'N SPOKES with questions about your order, call 1-888-888-2201.

Subscribe to SPORTS N SPOKES @ http://pvamag.com/sns/store/subscribe/
Opt-In for the digital issue beginning November 2014

Get Out & Enjoy Life

In 2011, we first introduced followers of our social media pages to the idea of exploring your world and sharing those experiences with us by submitting your outdoor sporting, recreation and travel pictures.

Since then, we've received hundreds of photos from people worldwide who get out and enjoy life each summer on wheels. You'll see many of those pictures on the upcoming pages within this book!

Now that we're in our fifth year of our accessible travel program, SPORTS 'N SPOKES, Wheel:Life, LASCI, and iPush Foundation have joined forces to highlight many accessible destinations across the United States and beyond. Please note that not every state in the US is featured in this travel guide, just the ones that we have included in our GOEL program to date.

We hope you will enjoy this listing of travel destinations that we have compiled over the last five years. We host program every year to help you broaden your horizons with ideas of what is waiting for you just up the road!

More Resources to Help You Get Out & Enjoy Life

One of the biggest challenges to planning a fantastic getaway is the cost, especially when you have accessibility needs or other considerations. If you are working with a limited budget or facing a financial challenge, feel free to download our complimentary Fundraising guide via the Wheel:Life website - http://wheel-life.org/book-request-form/.

Once you have a destination in mind, you might want to gather a group of friends to go with you! Looking for friends who travel on wheels too? Consider connecting with a local peer support group in your community.

Wheel:Life offers a free directory of peer support groups by state on our main website at http://wheel-life.org/connecting-peer-support-group-community/. We hope you'll get connected with new friends who are also wheelchair users in your hometown.

Ready? Let's go!

Alabama

"Beauty, history and adventure all come together in Alabama, a state rich in everything from world-class golf to white-sand beaches. It's a place where each meal is a celebration, each town has a story and each day brings new discoveries you'll always remember." (source: www.alabama.travel.com)

US Space & Rocket Center

More than 12 million people have visited Huntsville's U.S. Space and Rocket Center since it opened as NASA's first visitor center in 1970. A fully interactive museum loaded with exhibits about the past and future of space exploration, the space center is a blast for all ages. Here you'll find the world's largest museum dedicated to space – past, present, future. IMAX and 3D Theaters, Davidson Center for Space Exploration, and it's the home of Space Camp® and Aviation Challenge®.

Website: www.rocketcenter.com
Phone: 256-837-3400; 800-63-SPACE

Barber Motorsports Park

George Barber raced, modified, and maintained Porsches in the 1960's (63 first-place wins). He started collecting and restoring classic sports cars in 1989, but his interest soon turned to motorcycles. Mr. Barber recognized that there was not a museum which reflected the history of motorcycles around the world. So he made one!

Barber Motorsports Park in Birmingham has quickly become one of the most popular attractions in Alabama, especially among racing enthusiasts. The 17-turn, 2.38-mile road course is housed on a 740-acre, beautifully landscaped park that plays host to some of the Southeast's premier racing events. Don't forget to buy a ticket to the Barber Vintage Motorsports Museum, home to the world's best motorcycle collection.

Phone: 205-699-7275
Website: www.barbermuseum.org

Huntsville Botanical Garden

Huntsville Botanical Garden, a valuable community resource for education, recreation and entertainment, is open to the public year-round and is enjoyed by more than 350,000 visitors annually. Spread over 112 lush acres, the Huntsville Botanical Garden is open year-round and features an incredible variety of plant life. The beauty is all around as you make your way down the Dogwood Trail, find inspiration among the 14 themed herb gardens and gaze on a staggering 675 daylily varieties.

Website: http://www.hsvbg.org
Facebook: http://www.facebook.com/HuntsvilleBotanicalGarden

Alabama Vacation Guide

Whether you're planning a weekend of historical haunts or a seven-day beach getaway for the entire family, the Alabama Vacation Guide will help you round out your trip with the perfect mix of activities, attractions and accommodations. The guide contains information for the state's four diverse regions – North, Central, South and Gulf Coast – so no matter where you are in Alabama, you'll be prepared to experience and explore each area to the fullest.

Get your free copy at: http://www.alabama.travel/tourism-department/publications/vacation-guide/

Birmingham Zoo

"The Birmingham Zoo is Alabama's must-see attraction, drawing more than 575,000 visitors annually. Approximately 950 animals of 230 species call the 122-acre Birmingham Zoo home, including sea lions, rhinos and endangered species from six continents."

Website: http://www.birminghamzoo.com/plan-your-visit/zoo-map/
Phone: 205-879-0409
Facebook: https://www.facebook.com/BirminghamZoo

Red Mountain Park

"Red Mountain State Park offers trails and the Mega-Zip, an accessible zip-line that is appropriate for any ability level. A NOMAD (all terrain type of wheelchair) was recently donated to the park and is free to use if it is booked on the Red Mountain Park website."

Website: http://www.redmountainpark.org/
Phone: (205) 202-6043
Facebook: https://www.facebook.com/pages/Red-Mountain-Park/182530602646

Oak Mountain State Park

"The Alabama State Parks Division operates and maintains 22 state parks encompassing approximately 48,000 acres of land and water in Alabama. The parks range from Gulf Coast beaches to Appalachian Mountains providing opportunities and facilities from basic day-use activities to resort convention lodging, restaurant and golfing areas."

Websitehttp://www.alapark.com/oak-mountain-state-park
Phone: 1-800-ALA-PARK (252-7275)
Facebook: https://www.facebook.com/OakMountainSP

Aldridge Gardens

"Since Aldridge Gardens opened in 2002, the 30-acre former property of well-known horticulturist Eddie Aldridge and his wife Kay has become a popular attraction in the greater Birmingham area. The young garden showcases hydrangeas, including the Snowflake Hydrangea, which was patented by Mr. Aldridge and is now the official flower of the City of Hoover."

"Other features include an event venue and gallery in the couple's former home, an outdoor pavilion, a six-acre lake and a half-mile walking trail. The Gardens also host plant sales, art exhibits and shows, classes and seminars, bird walks, fishing days, concerts and more. Also, the tour of the Aldridge house and the majority of the walkways are accessible."

Website: http://aldridgegardens.com/home.html
Email: info@aldridgegardens.com
Facebook: https://www.facebook.com/pages/Aldridge-Gardens/169097700352?fref=ts

Alaska

"Alaska is different from every other destination in the world. Every day offers an unforgettable memory: a mother moose and calf, glaciers and mountains, unique Native cultures, our Russian legacy and Gold Rush days." – Governor Sean Parnell

Challenge Alaska Adaptive Ski and Snowboard School

"Challenge Alaska improves the quality of life for people with disabilities and the whole community through adaptive sports, therapeutic recreation, and education.
Since 1995, the Challenge has offered a variety of lessons at Alyeska Resort. Challenge Alaska is located slope side next to the beginner hill near the base of Bear Cub Quad."

Website: http://www.challengealaska.org/
Phone: 907-783-2925
Facebook: http://www.facebook.com/pages/Challenge-Alaska/118942348126005

Sea Wolf Adventures

"We offer small ship cruising adventures for everyone including wheelers and slow walkers. Everyone needs adventure and getting into a kayak and paddling through the wonders of nature is food for the soul. So come on one of our adventure cruises with us and see whales, bears, glaciers and amazing vistas in Glacier Bay National park, Alaska."

Website: http://www.seawolfadventures.net/accessadventure/index.html
Email: kimber@seawolfadventures.net
Phone: 907-957-1438

Alaska Railroad

"The Alaska Railroad stretches 470 miles from Seward on the south-central Kenai Peninsula, to the northern "golden heart" city of Fairbanks. Along the way, the train travels through some of the most scenic and rugged territory in Alaska, including Denali National Park, Denali State Park, and Chugach National Forest. The Alaska Railroad runs two primary passenger services during the summer season. On the rail north of Anchorage, the Denali Star operates daily between Fairbanks, Denali, Talkeetna and Anchorage. To the south, the Coastal Classic operates daily between Anchorage and Seward. The Alaska Railroad is accessible to wheelchairs, with special ramps at the depots and provisions on the train cars for occupied wheel chairs." (www.alaskatravel.com)

Website: http://www.alaskarailroad.com/
Phone: 907-265-2494
Email: reservations@akrr.com
Facebook: http://www.facebook.com/AlaskaRailroad

Jessica Piraino gets out and enjoys a new adventure with mom and dad skiing at spring break in Alaska. Photo courtesy of Get Out & Enjoy Life campaign.

Arizona

"Arizona is full of grand adventures, including outdoor recreation, site seeing, and more. Visit the Grand Canyon, or learn about American Indian Culture. The activities are endless." (source: http://visitarizona.com/)

Daring Adventures

"Daring Adventures is an exciting program that offers seven outdoor recreation opportunities for teens and adults with disabilities and their non-disabled peers. The programs are a great way to get active while meeting new people."

They Offer:
- ADAPTIVE CYCLING
- ADAPTIVE KAYAKING
- SLED ICE HOCKEY
- CROSS-COUNTRY SKIING
- HIKING
- BACKPACKING
- WILDERNESS CAMPING

Website: http://www.daring-adventures.org/

Sunrise Adaptive Sports

"SUNRISE ADAPTIVE SPORTS is working to make extraordinary things happen here in the White Mountains of Arizona. For the past 3 years, Sunrise Adaptive Sports has been working to change lives, or more accurately, show people that they have the power within themselves to change their own lives.

The mission of the Sunrise Adaptive Sports is to expand the potential of people with disabilities and special needs through meaningful, educational, and inspiring on-snow experiences. S.A.S. began back in 2009 with a group of volunteers only, donations from sponsors, and good, genuine intentions from all those involved. Now S.A.S. offers Adaptive Skiing and Snowboarding, we have scholarshipped several disabled skiers and boarders for all day private lessons at Sunrise Park Resort, we have paid for Sunrise Park Resort Ski School Employees to obtain much needed adaptive teaching certifications and schooling, and we have purchased the Sunrise Park Resort Adaptive Program a brand new, state of the art mono ski."
Website: http://www.sunriseadaptivesports.com/

Phone: 928-242-1329
Email: SunriseAdaptiveSports@gmail.com
Facebook: http://www.facebook.com/pages/Sunrise-Adaptive-Sports/124494870953071

Stagecoach Trails Guest Ranch

"Located in the heart of cowboy country, our guest ranch family is dedicated to providing you with the best dude ranch vacation you can find. We have worked hard to create a special, friendly atmosphere where you can get a glimpse into the old west while enjoying the beautiful NW Arizona desert and all the peace and quiet one could hope for. We invite you to stay with us and be part of our guest ranch family, even if it is only for a little while."

"We have a wheelchair ramp that enables all of our disabled guests the opportunity to ride. (Even our senior riders like to use it!) We can take them riding in the arena or out on trails and we provide side walkers for a safe and memorable ride. The family can go along on the rides too, which really makes it meaningful for our disabled guests and their families. There are no curbs, stairs or barriers either."

Website: http://www.stagecoachtrailsranch.com/docs/The%20Impossible%20Dream...Isn%27t.pdf
Email: vacation@stgr.com
Facebook: https://www.facebook.com/stagecoachtrailsranch

Bartlett Lake Marina

"Outdoor enthusiasts frequent Bartlett Lake for a variety of recreational opportunities, including shoreline camping in Arizona's natural desert terrain. While in this part of the Tonto National Forest, visitors may see mule deer, bald eagles, javelina, coyotes, and many indigenous desert plants, including the majestic saguaro, mesquite trees and blooming ocotillo.

Bartlett Lake is located only 48 miles from downtown Phoenix and 17 miles northeast of Carefree. The newly engineered, fully paved, scenic Bartlett Lake Road combined with the expanding Phoenix freeway system offers easy access from the entire Valley of the Sun. Tonto National Forest campground improvements, handicap accessibility, and safety features provide for safe, enjoyable recreation including hiking, boating, water skiing and fishing."

Website: http://www.bartlettlake.com/about.html
Email: Bryan@Bartlettlake.com
Facebook: https://www.facebook.com/bartlettlakemarina?sk=wall

Grand Canyon River Outfitters Association

"The Grand Canyon River Outfitters Association (GCROA) is a non-profit trade group made up of the sixteen professional river outfitters which are contracted with the National Park Service to provide the public with multi-day whitewater river trips within the Grand Canyon National Park. Each outfitter is anxious to share an experience of a lifetime with you!"

Website: http://www.gcroa.org/home.html
Email: john@gcroa.org
Facebook: https://www.facebook.com/gcriveroutfitters

California
(Northern)

"Discover miles of sun-drenched coast, an inviting ocean, and a year-round daily forecast of 70°F, and you'll understand why this state is all about outdoor fun. Visit Yosemite National park, or check out some of California's finest vineyards. With endless entertainment, attractions, Beaches and cities, California truly has it all." (source: www.visitcalifornia.com)

Bay Area Outreach and Recreation Program (BORP)

BORP is headquartered in Berkeley, California and is the leading provider and promoter of accessible sports and recreation opportunities for children and adults with physical disabilities in the greater San Francisco Bay Area. In addition to our high quality innovative sports and recreation programs, our expert staff provides advocacy, trainings, referrals and consultation services and have helped initiate adaptive sports programs in several other cities across the state. BORP also conducts disability awareness trainings and adaptive sports exhibitions for a variety of community agencies and serves as a valuable resource to physical therapists, rehabilitation hospitals, parks and recreation departments and related organizations.

Website: www.borp.org
Email: info@borp.org
Phone: 510-849-4663
Facebook: http://www.facebook.com/borp.org

Bay Area Association of Disabled Sailors

The Bay Area Association of Disabled Sailors (BAADS) seeks to make all aspects of sailing accessible. To fulfill this mission, we offer dinghy sailing every Saturday and keelboat sailing every Sunday out of South Beach Marina, adjacent to AT&T Park.

Our keelboat fleet includes four keelboats, each specially rigged and equipped with adaptive features to make sailing the San Francisco Bay possible for people with disabilities. Additionally, we have 23 Access Dinghies, ranging in size from 8 to 14 feet long, all of which are specifically designed for people with disabilities. Some of these are equipped with servo motors so that people with severe physical disabilities can sail solo.

Website: www.baads.org
Phone: 415-281-0212
Email: info@baads.org
Facebook: https://www.facebook.com/BAADSSF

Environmental Traveling Companions (ETC)

ETC opens the beauty and challenge of the great outdoors to people with disabilities and disadvantaged youth. Every year, more than 2,000 people join ETC to raft whitewater rivers, ski alpine meadows, kayak the waters of the Golden Gate and Tomales Bay, and build leadership skills.

Website: www.etctrips.org
Phone: (415) 474-7662
Facebook: http://www.facebook.com/ETCtrips

Access Leisure & Paralympics Sport Sacramento Club

Access Leisure is a program of the City of Sacramento Department of Parks and Recreation. Access Leisure provides sports, residential camping and outdoor education as well as social and fitness programs for children, teens, and adults with disabilities.

Website: http://www.accessleisuresac.org
Email: jyarrow@cityofsacramento.org
Phone: (916) 808-3809

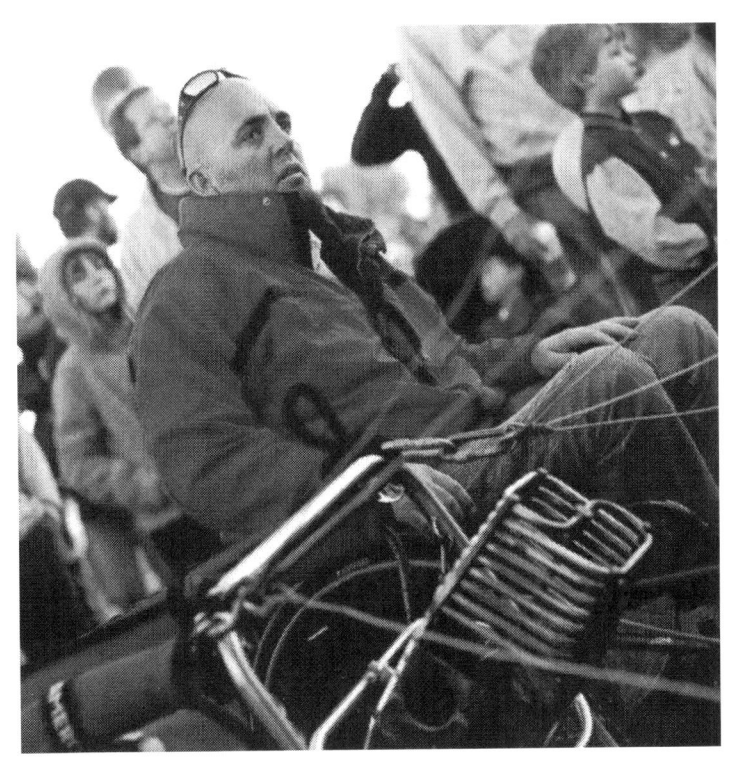

Michael Glen makes the most of life by flying hot air balloons across the country. Photo Courtesy of Get Out & Enjoy Life Campaign.

Up & Away

"In Spring 2011, Up & Away Ballooning became the first hot air balloon operator in the United States to offer wheelchair adventurers the opportunity to soar above the magnificent hills and vineyards of the Sonoma County Wine County. The Pegasus Project's specially-designed and crafted passenger basket makes it possible for wheelchair users, to break the bounds and float away on the gentle winds."

"The special basket with a lowered rail, easy access ramp and window makes it possible for the seated passenger to enjoy more than 180-degree visibility."

Website: http://www.up-away.com/wheelchair.html
Email: flightinfo@up-away.com

Wheeling California's Coast

"California's spectacular coast offers many outdoor adventures for wheelchair riders, parents pushing strollers, and others who need accessibility features such as a wide, fairly level and firm path of travel. This guide can help you choose the destinations that suit your needs from among the coast's many wheelchair-accessible parks, trails, beaches, viewpoints, and other sites of interest."

Website: http://www.wheelingcalscoast.org/
Facebook: https://www.facebook.com/wheelingcalscoast

Bay Nature

The Bay Nature Institute, based in Berkeley, California, is dedicated to educating the people of the San Francisco Bay Area about, and celebrating the beauty of, the surrounding natural world. We do so with the aim of inspiring residents to explore and preserve the diverse and unique natural heritage of the region, and of nurturing productive relationships among the many organizations and individuals working towards these same goals.

Website: https://baynature.org/articles/got-wheels/
Email: webmaster@baynature.org
Facebook: https://www.facebook.com/BayNature

Reach for the Stars

"Reach for the Stars Hot Air Balloon Foundation is a California non-profit corporation based in Riverside County and is recognized by the IRS as a federal 501c3 corporation. Our mission is to share the joy and excitement of hot air ballooning with all people, especially those with physical challenges."

"Our unique, easy-entry custom baskets allow people with limited mobility, as well as wheelchair users, to experience a tethered ride or a traditional flight."

Website: http://reach4thestars.org/about-us/
Phone: 951-538-7368
Facebook: https://www.facebook.com/reachforthestarshotairballoon

(Southern)

California Coastal Commission – Beach Wheelchairs

This website showcases several coastal cities in California that offer beach wheelchair rentals. The special wheels are able to roll across the sand without sinking. All of the beaches listed on this website provide beach wheelchairs free of charge. The California Coastal Commission is committed to serve ALL residents of the state and ensure their beach experience is wonderful.

Website: http://www.coastal.ca.gov/access/beach-wheelchairs.html
Email: coast4u@coastal.ca.gov

Disneyland

Just like Disney World in Orlando, Disneyland in Anaheim, California is fully accessible to people with disabilities. Disneyland is accessible to those with hearing and visual disabilities as well as mobility. Service animals are welcome too! Come make your dreams come true at the magical Disneyland in Anaheim, California.

Website: http://disneyland.disney.go.com/plan/guest-services/guests-with-disabilities/
Facebook: http://www.facebook.com/Disneyland
Phone: (714) 781-4565

Accessible San Diego

This is an extremely helpful website for travelers with disabilities. It is a non-profit information center that serves as a guide for accessible hotels, tours, lift transportation and attractions. This guide of the San Diego area provides news, event information, travel guides and more!

Website: http://www.asd.travel/
Facebook: www.facebook.com/pages/Accessible-San-Diego/104542773907
Email: mail@asd.travel

U.S.S. Midway Museum

This is an experience of a lifetime! Experience life at sea on one of America's longest serving aircraft carriers. Visitors will walk (or roll) in the footsteps of 225,000 Midway sailors who have served our country. Accessibility is always a priority here. There are complimentary wheelchair rentals as well as elevator access onto the ship and inside the ship.

Website: http://www.midway.org/wheelchair
Facebook: http://www.facebook.com/ussmidwaymuseum
Phone: 619-544-9600

Discover Los Angeles For Disabled Visitors

This thorough website is an excellent guide for people with disabilities who want to travel to Los Angeles. It lists LA's top accessible attractions which include but are not limited to; aquariums, arts and music, attractions, entertainment, landmarks, museums, gardens, and transportation. Check out Discover Los Angeles and see which accessible activity best suits you!

Website: http://discoverlosangeles.com/guides/la-living/active-la/la-for-disabled-visitors.html

Ability First

"Through 25 locations across Southern California, Ability First provides programs for children and adults with disabilities and special needs services to help participants reach their full potential throughout their lives. We offer a broad range of employment, recreational and socialization special needs programs and operate 12 accessible residential housing complexes."

"Most Ability First programs qualify for funding through the state-supported Regional Centers. However, government support provides only about half of the dollars necessary to deliver high quality programs and services. As a nonprofit organization, we rely heavily on the generous support of hundreds of donors who share our vision."

Website: http://www.abilityfirst.org/index.aspx
Email: info@abilityfirst.org
Facebook: https://www.facebook.com/AbilityFirst

LEGOLAND

"With more than 60 rides, shows and attractions it's an interactive, hands-on theme park experience for families with children 2-12. The Resort is also home to SEA LIFE® Aquarium and the world's first LEGOLAND Water Park. And if you've ever dreamed of spending the night at LEGOLAND, LEGOLAND Hotel at the Resort is now open and less than 2 miles from the nearest beach!"

Website: http://california.legoland.com/FAQ/disabled_access/
Email: experience@LEGOLAND.com.
Facebook: https://www.facebook.com/legolandcalifornia

Wheelchair Lacrosse USA

"WLUSA is the governing body of Wheelchair Lacrosse in the United States. We offer information on how you can join a team or start a team and make an impact."

Website: http://www.wheelchairlacrosse.com/
Email: info@wheelchairlacrosse.com
Facebook: https://www.facebook.com/pages/Wheelchair-Lacrosse-USA/318438884517?ref=hl

Colorado

"Mountains were made to move you. Come remember what freedom feels like. And forget that traffic jams and spreadsheets even exist. Go farther than you've ever gone before. From this vantage point, you can see everything except limits. Colorado isn't just a place to visit. It's a place where you feel alive." (source: www.colorado.com)

Wilderness on Wheels

Wilderness On Wheels Foundation was established as a not-for-profit corporation in March of 1986. Its mission: Stimulate the development of access for disabled persons to natural outdoor environments. The approach to the mission: Construct a model wilderness-access facility. First, to learn how and then to share that information with anyone, anywhere, and anytime. The goal for the model facility: Install an 8-foot wide boardwalk starting at 9,100 feet to the top of a 12,300 foot mountain.

Website: http://www.wildernessonwheels.org/
Phone: (303) 403-1110
Email: wildernessonwheels@gmail.com

Sports Made Possible

"There is something about playing the game of baseball that lights up the eyes of a child, however for children facing physical and/or mental challenges, that opportunity is often not available. Adaptive Baseball gives these children the opportunity to get out and enjoy playing the game of baseball in its purest form. During each game, every child is given an opportunity to hit the ball and score a run. Team members are assigned "buddies" who assist them in hitting the ball and "running" the bases. Buddies can be fellow schoolmates, parents, college students, business leaders or anyone who wishes to volunteer their time to give a child the gift of baseball.

The point of the game is less about baseball and more about fun! The benefits gained by everyone involved are tremendous. The child's self esteem grows, they make friends, become less isolated and "just become a regular kid, not a kid with a disability."

Website: http://www.sportsmadepossible.org/

The Breckenridge Outdoor Education Center

"The BOEC was established in Breckenridge, Colorado, in 1976 as a non-profit tax-exempt educational organization to provide outdoor experiences for people with disabilities and to train the instructors who work with special populations. Ultimately, the BOEC strives to integrate disability with ability, providing outdoor experiences to all. We welcome people of all abilities from around the world to spectacular natural classrooms in the Rocky Mountains and beyond."

Website: http://www.boec.org/
Phone: 970.453.6422
Email: boec@boec.org
Facebook: http://www.facebook.com/pages/Breckenridge-Outdoor-Education-Center/349984009510

Adaptive Adventures

"Adaptive Adventures is now in its 12th year of creating life changing opportunities for people with physical disabilities. Adaptive Adventures opens the doors to hope and allows people to realize their dreams. Program participants enjoy fresh air, rushing water, and abundant sunshine as they glide down ski slopes, cut through the water in a kayak or wakeboard, or bike through the Rocky Mountains and along the shores of Lake Michigan."

Website: http://adaptiveadventures.org/
Phone: 303.396.1339
Email: info@adaptiveadventures.org

Adaptive Sports Center

"The Adaptive Sports Center enhances the quality of life of people with disabilities through exceptional outdoor adventure activities. The successful programs the ASC provides are inclusive to families and friends, empower our participants in their daily lives and have a positive enduring effect on self-efficacy, health, independence and overall well-being."

Website: http://www.adaptivesports.org/
Facebook: https://www.facebook.com/pages/Adaptive-Sports-Center/133745759970333?sk=wall

Craig Hospital's Adventure Program

"Craig Hospital's Adventure Program offers unique opportunities for travel, sports and outdoor recreation. We offer a range of activities for alumni and current patients including scuba diving, hand cycling, fishing, hunting and horseback riding."

"Our programs range from local cycling races to exotic trips like Belize to scuba dive. We've gone horseback riding in the Rocky Mountains and taken cruises to the Caribbean and Alaska. The powerful impact of this program brings together newly injured individuals and alumni to create lasting friendships and peer relationships."

Website: https://craighospital.org/programs/therapeutic-recreation/adventure-alumni-programs
Phone: 303-789-8000
Facebook: https://www.facebook.com/craighospital?fref=ts

Delaware

"Here, bustling boardwalks lead to sandy beaches and the soothing sounds of surf. Shady walkways weave through gardens perfumed with blossoms at elegant du Pont mansions. From north to south, Delaware streets lead to chic shopping centers, boutique-blessed towns and designer outlet malls – perfect for saving with tax-free shopping."

Step-by-step trails lead you to Delaware's best in dining, local wineries and breweries, historic sites and outdoor wonders. Choose from paths that are well-worn, or make your own. Delaware's year-round events, rich history and natural beauty offer so much to do that the tough part is deciding where to begin." (source: http://www.visitdelaware.com/)

Rehoboth Beach

"It is a place where people can stroll down tree-lined streets, neighbors know one another, children play outside and a diverse community comes together to preserve the city's charm and unique character. There is even a Beach Wheels program, making Rehoboth Beach even more accessible."

Website: http://www.cityofrehoboth.com/visitors/beach-and-boardwalk/handicap-beach-access#
Phone: 302-227-2280
Facebook: https://www.facebook.com/pages/Rehoboth-Beach/223035505943

Longwood Gardens

"Our Gardens are a living expression of all that our founder, Pierre S. du Pont, found inspiring, meaningful, and beautiful. From the intricate fountain systems to the meticulous gardens to the architectural grandeur, awe-inspiring discoveries await at every turn. Most garden paths are wide and paved, and a wheelchair route is suggested on the Guide Map."

Website: http://longwoodgardens.org/visit/special-needs
Email: questions@longwoodgardens.org
Facebook: https://www.facebook.com/LongwoodGardens

Nemours Mansion and Gardens

"There are a variety of surfaces and levels in the garden and grounds. Tours are two and half to three hours in duration. All guests must be 12 years of age or older. The Mansion is ADA accessible but please be aware that the gardens are not. However, they can be viewed and enjoyed by bus."

Website: http://www.nemoursmansion.org/content/nemours/mansion/visit.html
Email: tours@nemours.org

Riverfront Wilmington

"Riverfront Wilmington is one of the most exciting redevelopment stories in the nation. Located halfway between New York City and Washington D.C., Wilmington is an up-and-coming cosmopolitan city that is attracting major employers, restaurant, entrepreneurial ventures and exciting residential developments. A significant part of this success story is the Christina Riverfront, which has been transformed from a polluted, industrial wasteland into a thriving destination enjoyed by people of all ages. Riverfront Wilmington combines its rich history with a host of new attractions that bring great food, entertainment, and shopping to our city."

Website: http://www.riverfrontwilm.com/
Email: info@riverfrontwilm.com
Facebook: https://www.facebook.com/riverfrontwilm?fref=ts

Air Mobility Command Museum

"The museum houses over 30 aircraft varying in roles and sizes. Cargo haulers, fighters, helicopters, a presidential aircraft, and even a bomber; the museum has a little bit of everything! Learn about the humanitarian and war efforts the men and women undertook to help aid those in need and support the U.S. military."

Website: http://amcmuseum.org/
Email: amcmuseum@us.af.mil
Facebook: https://www.facebook.com/AMCMuseum

Florida

"The state of Florida is known around the world for its white sandy beaches and many exciting Florida attractions! As the land of endless summer, it's no surprise that Florida is home to more attractions than anywhere else in the U.S. Whether you're a visitor or a home grown Floridian, you'll love the variety and quality of these magical and sometimes unique destinations." (source: http://www.floridatourism.com/)

Linda Lamberth and her grandson Zach enjoying Clearwater Beach, Florida. Picture courtesy of 2014 Get Out, Enjoy Life campaign.

Walt Disney World

Walt Disney World is the most magical place in the world! It is the land of Mickey and Minnie Mouse, The Disney Princesses, "It's a Small World After All", and the giant Mickey Mouse ears ice cream bars. It is where dreams come true. Dreams will come true for anyone here, even for those with disabilities. Walt Disney World is committed to provide for as many guests as possible, so there are specific accommodations for those with hearing, mobility and visual disabilities. Service animals are allowed as well. For more information, please visit the Walt Disney World website and check out their Facebook page.

Website: http://disneyworld.disney.go.com/guests-with-disabilities/
Facebook: http://www.facebook.com/#!/WaltDisneyWorld
Phone: 407-824-4321

Dolphin Research Center

The Special Needs Pathways Program at the Dolphin Research Center assists and enables individuals with disabilities to interact with dolphins and sea lions. This organization provides private workshops, specialized equipment and in-water or on-dock assistance depending on the adult or child's disability.

Website: http://www.dolphins.org/visit_special_needs.php
Facebook: http://www.facebook.com/#!/DolphinResearchCenter
Phone: 305-289-1121
email: joan@dolphins.org

Florida Aquarium

Explore one of the most magnificent attractions in downtown Tampa at the Florida Aquarium. This is a family friendly spot that is fully accessible. There are even wheelchair rentals available and several handicapped parking spaces.

Website: http://www.flaquarium.org/explore-the-aquarium/accessibility.aspx
Facebook: http://www.facebook.com/#!/florida.aquarium.tampa
Phone: 813-273-4000

Florida Disabled Outdoors Association

The Florida Disabled Outdoors Association is a non-profit 501(c)(3) organization that strives to enrich lives with accessible recreation for all. Health and wellness is always promoted through several programs such as SportsAbility, Recreation Activity Program for Adults with Disabilities, Brain and Spinal Cord Injury Resources, ALLOUT Adventure Program, and Miracle Sports.

Website: http://www.fdoa.org/
Facebook: http://www.facebook.com/#!/fdoa.org
Phone: 850-201-2944

Rock Bottom Divers

Rock Bottom Divers is a scuba diving charter and instruction organization that provides rehabilitation to wounded military veterans. You will meet Scott Crawford, who has been a Handicapped Scuba Association Open Water Instructor for 20 years. You will dive off Rock Bottom's vessel in the beautiful Gulf of Mexico.

Website: http://rockbottomdivers.net/disabled-divers.html
Facebook: http://www.facebook.com/#!/RockBottomDivers
Phone: 855-448-7625

Miami Heat Wheels

"The Miami Heat Wheels is a competitive wheelchair basketball team in the National Wheelchair Basketball Association (NWBA). Competing at the Division III level in the Florida Wheelchair Basketball Conference, the adult wheelchair basketball team competes in local and regional competitions associated with the the NWBA."

"The Heat Wheels continue to excite everyone from South Florida and around the country. Inspired by the recent and dominating presence of great players such as Carlos Ocasio and Ricardo Lucien, the members of the Heat Wheels are to broaden their commitment to the community through service, athletics, and fine citizenship."

Website: http://www.miamiheatwheels.com/
Facebook: https://www.facebook.com/heatwheels?fref=ts

Georgia

"If outdoor adventures excite you, then you'll love the pristine beaches along Georgia's coast, scenic hiking trails, the refreshing scenery of the north Georgia mountains, gorgeous lakes, wildlife refuges, camping, fresh water and salt water fishing, one of the country's best state parks systems, great year-round golf, or whitewater rafting. Georgia has some of the top amusement parks and attractions in the world, and in the beautiful Georgia mountains, the Georgia Wine Highway hosts many special events that will please the palate." (source: http://www.georgiatouristguide.com/)

Jacob's Ladder Riding

"The mission of Jacobs' Ladder Therapeutic Riding Center is to provide equine related activities to individuals with special needs. Children as young as 3 years old may participate, as well as adults who desire to strengthen their physical bodies, build their self-esteem, gain a sense of independence, learn new skills & make new friends."

Website: http://www.jacobsladderriding.com/
Phone: (229)794-1188
Email: leslie_j@hotmail.com

BlazeSports

"Driven by a desire to provide all children and adults with physical disabilities the chance to play sports and live healthy, active lives, BlazeSports is dedicated to offering programs, education and tools worldwide."

Website: http://www.blazesports.org/
Phone: 404-270-2000
Facebook: http://www.facebook.com/blazesports

Camp Twin Lakes

"Camp Twin Lakes is a network of camps providing life-changing camp experiences to thousands of Georgia's children with serious illnesses, disabilities and other challenges each year. We collaborate with over 50 different organizations each serving a different population, to create customized programs that teach our campers to overcome obstacles and grow in their confidence and capabilities. Camp Twin Lakes is thrilled to provide programs at various state-of-the-art locations throughout the state of Georgia, including camps in Rutledge, Winder, Warm Springs, children's hospitals, and more."

Website: http://www.camptwinlakes.org/
Phone: 404-231-9887
Email: contact@camptwinlakes.org
Facebook: http://www.facebook.com/camptwinlakes

The Georgia Aquarium

Journey with Gentle Giants is the only opportunity in the world where you are guaranteed to swim with whale sharks, the largest fish in the world, in Georgia Aquarium's Ocean Voyager exhibit built by The Home Depot. Guests will swim at the surface with a floatation device and air supplied by either a small compressed air cylinder or a snorkel. The following equipment is provided: mask and snorkel, gloves, booties, wetsuit, floatation device and compressed air cylinder. Personal masks are permitted. The entire Dive Immersion Team is certified by the Handicapped Scuba Association as either Divemasters or Instructors. Anyone with or without disabilities who is a certified open water diver is invited to purchase the SCUBA dive, and anyone with or without disabilities desiring to snorkel is invited to purchase the snorkel option. Note: Changing areas have limited accommodations. Please let us know in advance if you have specific needs or if you use mobility equipment.

Website: http://www.georgiaaquarium.org/plan-your-visit/accessability.aspx
Phone: 404.581.4000

Casimir Chester meets a Beluga whale at the Georgia Aquarium. Picture courtesy of 2015 Get Out, Enjoy Life campaign.

Six Flags

"We strive to safely accommodate the needs of all guests including guests with disabilities. Wheelchairs and electric convenience vehicles are available for rent just inside Orleans Place, on a first-come, first-served basis. There is a fee as well as a refundable deposit to rent these items. Please note that Segways are not permitted in the park."

Website: https://www.sixflags.com/overgeorgia/plan-your-visit/park-services pdf

Facebook: https://www.facebook.com/sixflagsovergeorgia

Shepherd Center

"Shepherd Center incorporates recreation therapy and activity into your rehabilitation program to improve self esteem, relieve stress and increase mobility. Shepherd Center's Health and Wellness Hands-On Clinic is aimed to individuals with a spinal cord injury, C-6 or below. Participants will receive continued education to learn, review and practice wheelchair sports, such as hand cycling and wheelchair tennis.

Website: http://www.shepherd.org/resources/sports-recreation
Email: admissions@shepherd.org.
Facebook: https://www.facebook.com/shepherdcenter

Hawaii

"The fresh, floral air energizes you. The warm, tranquil waters refresh you. The breathtaking, natural beauty renews you. Look around. There's no place on earth like Hawaii. Whether you're a new visitor or returning, our six unique islands offer distinct experiences that will entice any traveler." (source: http://www.gohawaii.com/)

KORE Kauai

"We are a grassroots, volunteer driven, non-profit organization under the umbrella of the Kauai YMCA. We are dedicated to helping both Kauai residents and visitors who are physically challenged or have special needs to get back into the ocean with the assistance of trained professionals. Whether it be surfing or just relaxing in the water, our intent is to get our residents and their families to once again enjoy a day at the beach."

Website: www.korekauai.com
Phone: 808-651-6416
Facebook: http://www.facebook.com/korekauai
Email: KOREKauai@hotmail.com

Sunshine Helicopters

If you thought helicopter tours were out of your reach, think again. Thanks to Sunshine Helicopters' special lift, you can see the splendor of Maui, Oahu, Kauai, and the Big Island from the sky.

Website: www.sunshinehelicopters.com
Email: bookings@sunshinehelicopters.com
Phone: 866-501-7738

Aquatic Adventures

Certified Divers can enjoy Hawaii's underwater beauty. One of our favorite dive sites is perfect for assisting disabled divers. And, once you get underwater, you'll enjoy some of the most beautiful and unique aquatic life in the Pacific.

Website: http://www.aascuba.com/pages/fun.htm
Phone: 808-645-0927

All-Terrain Wheelchairs

The Landeez All-Terrain Wheelchair is available free of charge for persons with disabilities through the Honolulu Parks and Recreation.

Website: http://www.honolulu.gov/parks/dprtru.html
Phone: (808) 768-3027
Email: parks-tru@honolulu.gov

Access Aloha Van Rentals

Access Aloha Van Rentals offers U-Drive wheelchair and scooter vans on a daily, weekly, monthly or long term rental basis on the island of Oahu. Sales of new or used accessible vehicles are available, please inquire.

Website: http://www.accessalohatravel.com/accessiblevanrentals/

Tony Vindetti shares this picture from his first trip to HAWAII with his mom, along with an aunt, an uncle and sister on Oahu. He says, "Just to be out of my chair & feel the warm water from the waves splash over my head was so amazing!" Photo courtesy of Get Out & Enjoy Life campaign.

Idaho

"Scenic wonders await your exploration in Idaho. Take in awe-inspiring peaks, geological formations, lush green forests, and a waterfall higher than Niagara." (source: http://www.visitidaho.org/)

Cooperative Wilderness Handicapped Outdoor Group

The Cooperative Wilderness Handicapped Outdoor Group, otherwise known as CW HOG, is a regional self-help group that was formed in 1981 to provide recreational opportunities for people of all abilities.

Website: http://www.isu.edu/outdoor/cwhog.shtml
Facebook: https://www.facebook.com/pages/CW-HOG/198747786829296?sk=timeline

Sun Valley Adaptive Sports

"As a positive and visible fixture in the community, our programs give children, teens, adults, and veterans with disabilities the opportunity to experience competition and the outdoors without limitations. Designed and executed by our staff of certified therapists, each program helps our participants build physical and social skills they can take with them for a lifetime. What sets SVAS apart from other adaptive sports organizations across the country is our focus on innovative and sustainable therapeutic impact. While we want our participants to have a great time, we ensure the positive changes they experience translate to every aspect of their lives."

Website: http://www.svasp.org/
Phone: (208) 726-9298

SAIL

"SAIL (Self Awareness In Leisure) is a not for profit accessible sailing program designed for those with physical disabilities, ie. for individuals with spinal cord injuries, amputation(s), etc. We call our sailing program accessible versus disabled because our participants are willing to learn to sail, even if they need to find a different way; they are not letting a diagnosed disability, etc. limit them. We simply give them the tools so they can sail. Our first goal is not to make our participants dependent on us/a program but to assist them to become as independent as possible in sailing."

Website: http://funtosail.blogspot.com/p/disabled.html
Phone: 208-704-4454
Email: info@funtosail.com

Adventure Island Playground

"Adventure Island is a Universally Accessible Playground located in Meridian's Settler's Park at Meridian and Ustick Roads."

Website: http://www.adventureislandplayground.org/
Phone: 208-887-3531

Higher Ground Sun Valley

"At Higher Ground Sun Valley (HG), we enhance quality of life through inclusive therapeutic recreation and education for people of all abilities. As a positive and visible fixture in the adaptive recreation industry, our programs give individuals with disabilities the opportunity to experience competition and the outdoors without limitations. Designed and executed by our staff of certified therapists and dedicated professionals, each program helps our participants build physical and social skills they can use for a lifetime."

Website: http://www.highergroundsv.org/
Phone: (208) 726-9298
Facebook: https://www.facebook.com/HigherGroundSunValley

Illinois

"From the Magnificent Mile and Route 66 to wine trails and scenic byways, Illinois offers a wide variety of destinations for your next tour." (source: http://www.tourillinois.org/)

Rockford Park District – Indoor Sports Center, Loves Park
This indoor sports center contains three multi-sport indoor fields for soccer, volleyball, basketball, locker rooms, a sports store, and Skybox, a family-friendly restaurant and sports bar. Wheelchair sports are extremely popular at ISC. There is wheelchair basketball, power soccer and Blaze sports (track, field, bocce, basketball, and open gym) for children and adults who are in a wheelchair, are visually impaired, are amputees, or have a neurological/muscular impairment. The entire facility is handicapped accessible and there is adaptive equipment available for rental.
Website: http://www.rockfordparkdistrict.org/index.php/facilities/athletics/indoor-sports-center
Phone: 815-885-1135
Facebook: http://www.facebook.com/#!/rockfordparkdistrict

Michael Mills pushes harder through the 2014 BattleFrog Obstacle Course Race. Photo courtesy of Get Out & Enjoy Life campaign.

Great Lakes Adaptive Sports Association

The GLASA's motto is "Let no one sit on the sidelines". They serve children and adults with any type of physical or visual impairments which include but are not limited to: spinal cord injury, Spina Bifida, Cerebral Palsy, amputation, and muscular dystrophy. Participants can be ambulatory or be in a wheelchair. There are several events that range from golfing to weightlifting. To see what else the GLASA offers, please visit their website and Facebook page.
Website: http://glasa.org/index.php
Facebook: http://www.facebook.com/#!/GLASASports
Phone: 847-283-0908

Navy Pier, Chicago

Navy Pier works hard to ensure that their complex accommodates all types of disabilities. Entrances, elevators, telephones and services are all handicapped accessible. For over ten years, Navy Pier has been a tourist hot-spot and is the perfect place to enjoy a beautiful day on Lake Michigan.

Website: https://navypier.com/?s=disability+services
Facebook: http://www.facebook.com/#!/navypier
Phone: (312) 595-PIER

Chicago Indoor Rowing (Adaptive)

Participate in an open 1K or a 500 meter race with no prior experience! You can also compete in races such as The Arms Race and The Wounded Warrior Challenge. There are also adaptive seats that will suit you depending on your injury/mobility. There is a legs, trunk and arms seat, a trunk and arms seat and an arms only seat. This is a great way to stay active, no matter what type of impairment you have!

Video: http://www.youtube.com/watch?feature=player_embedded&v=NttlP7uYwFo
Website: http://www.chicagoindoorrowing.com/adaptiveb.htm
Phone: (507) 867-3961

USTA Adaptive Tennis, Northern Illinois

Come learn how to play tennis no matter what your disability is! There are tennis programs for all disabilities—everything from cognitive to physical disabilities. Come serve up some aces with the United States Tennis Association in Northern Illinois.

Website: http://www.northernillinois.usta.com/Adaptive_Tennis/Adaptive_Tennis/
Facebook: http://www.facebook.com/#!/USTANorthernIllinois
Phone: (914) 696-7000 (corporate)

Abilities Expo Chicago

"For more than 30 years, Abilities Expo has been the go-to source for the Community of people with disabilities, their families, seniors, veterans and healthcare professionals. Every event opens your eyes to new technologies, new possibilities, new solutions and new opportunities to change your life."

Website: http://www.abilities.com/chicago/
Facebook: https://www.facebook.com/AbilitiesExpo

Indiana

"There are so many things to do during an Honest-to-Goodness Indiana getaway, so come for a day, a weekend or longer. If you're looking for family travel, you'll love our museums, zoos, state parks and sports. Planning a girlfriend getaway? Check out our unique shopping venues, from popular outlet malls with designer clothing to local artisan and antique shops. If romance is in the air, see what's playing at a theater, meander an Indiana wine trail, hit the links or try your luck at a casino." (source: https://visitindiana.com)

Holiday World

Holiday World in rural Indiana has been voted the most family-friendly theme park in the USA for several years – at a much lower cost than other theme parks.

Website: http://www.holidayworld.com/help-information/accessibility/
Facebook: https://www.facebook.com/HolidayWorld?sid=b660a4148829021a9b66f8005420e3c1&ref=search

Indianapolis Motor Speedway and Hall of Fame Museum

"The Hall of Fame Museum, located five miles northwest of downtown Indianapolis on the grounds of the famous Indianapolis Motor Speedway, is recognized as one of the most highly visible museums in the world devoted to automobiles and auto racing. In 1987, the Speedway grounds were honored with the designation of National Historic Landmark."

Website: http://www.indianapolismotorspeedway.com/at-the-track/museum#
Phone: (317) 492-8500
Facebook: https://www.facebook.com/IndianapolisMotorSpeedway

Fort Wayne Children's Zoo

"The Fort Wayne Children's Zoo is operated by the non-profit Fort Wayne Zoological Society under a cooperative agreement with the Fort Wayne Parks and Recreation Department. Our mission is connecting kids and animals, strengthening families and inspiring people to care. The Fort Wayne Children's Zoo wishes to meet the needs of every visitor, so all areas of the zoo are stroller, wagon and wheelchair accessible."

Website: http://kidszoo.org/
Email: zmail@kidszoo.org
Facebook: https://www.facebook.com/kidszoo

Foellinger-Freimann Botanical Conservatory

"Always in Season: Surround yourself with nature at the Foellinger-Freimann Botanical Conservatory ~ an oasis in the heart of downtown Fort Wayne Indiana. Visit the Showcase Garden with its lush seasonal displays, wander through the Tropical Garden where orchids and palms thrive in the shadows of a cascading waterfall, or retreat to the quiet beauty of the Desert Garden."

Website: http://www.botanicalconservatory.org/
Phone: (260) 427-6440

Facebook: https://www.facebook.com/ConservatoryFW

Noah Barbknecht, 16 years old, T8 complete paraplegic competing at the Stueben County Youth Hunt in Indiana. Noah was the only youth using a bow, and the only one that harvested a turkey. Photo courtesy of Get Out & Enjoy Life campaign.

Iowa

"From fascinating museums and historic sites to theme parks and art galleries, Iowa offers attractions galore. Not to mention, the endless dining experiences available. Feast on Iowa's dining options - from mom 'n pop diners to chefs featuring locally-grown ingredients on their menus." (source: http://www.traveliowa.com/)

Jonathan Litzkow racing at the 2013 Taylor Morris Glow Run 5k in Cedar Falls, Iowa. Picture courtesy of 2014 Get Out, Enjoy Life campaign.

Adaptive Sports Iowa

"Our programs cater to the unique skill sets of athletes with physical disabilities all across our state. You can try out wheelchair basketball, beep baseball, be a part of our RAGBRAI team or hit the slopes in our Winter Experience!"

"Our goal is to bring fun, excitement, exercise and achieve a higher quality of life to the amazing athletes with physical disabilities in Iowa. And the best part is that we take everyone, from beginners to seasoned pros!"

Website: https://www.adaptivesportsiowa.org/
Phone: 888-777-8881
Facebook: https://www.facebook.com/adaptivesportsiowa

Dubuque Arboretum

"Established in 1980, the Dubuque Arboretum & Botanical Gardens in Marshall Park is a living museum developed by volunteers. Their work is a labor of love for all who visit The Gardens as well as a symbol of devotion for the growing things of the earth."

Website: http://www.dubuquearboretum.net/
Phone: 563.556.2100
Facebook: https://www.facebook.com/pages/Dubuque-Arboretum-Botanical-Gardens/152070251476128

Field of Dreams Movie Site

"In 1988, the Lansing Family Farm exchanged its humble roots for a destiny very few could have imagined. However, the story only begins there. Not long after the film's release, believers shaped, molded, and lovingly preserved what Hollywood and a brilliant novel had set in motion that previous year. The title, later changed to "Field of Dreams," has gained world-renowned accolades not only in film, but also as a beloved tourist destination for young and old alike."

Website: http://www.fodmoviesite.com/
Email: info@fodmoviesite.com
Facebook: https://www.facebook.com/FieldOfDreamsMovieSite

Living History Farms

"Living History Farms in Urbandale, Iowa, tells the amazing story of how Iowans transformed the fertile prairies of the Midwest into the most productive farmland in the world. While at the 500-acre open-air museum, visitors travel at their own pace through historical time periods spanning 300 years. On-site interpreters provide a unique learning environment of seasonal activities and demonstrations."

Website: http://www.lhf.org/
Phone: 515-278-5286
Facebook: https://www.facebook.com/LivingHistoryFarms

National Balloon Museum

"The National Balloon Museum dedicates itself to providing the public with a comprehensive understanding of ballooning and its history through its exhibitions and collections. The museum archives more than 200 years of ballooning, hosts 10,000 visitors a year (with 20 countries in attendance) and operates on more than 2,000 volunteer hours annually."

Website: http://www.nationalballoonmuseum.com/Home.aspx
Phone: (515) 961-3714
Facebook: https://www.facebook.com/pages/National-Balloon-Museum-Inc/135470023406

Kentucky

"From the rolling bluegrass-covered hills of legendary Horse Country and the grandstands of America's most storied thoroughbred racing tracks to the Kentucky Bourbon Trail and world-renowned outdoor adventure, visit Kentucky and experience the unbridled spirit that runs wild in the Bluegrass State." (source: Kentuckytourism.com)

CKRH Riding for Hope

"Central Kentucky Riding for Hope is dedicated to enriching the community by improving the quality of life and the health of children and adults with special physical, cognitive, emotional and social needs through therapeutic activities with the horse." They offer equine assisted activities & therapies, therapeutic riding, hippo therapy and more.
Website: www.ckrh.org
Phone: 859-231-7066

Iroquois Park Accessible Playground

The playground includes:

- AN ELABORATE PLAY AREA FOR CHILDREN AGES 5-12, CONNECTED BY RAMPS AND ELEVATED DECKS.
- A FENCED "TOT LOT" DESIGNED FOR CHILDREN AGES 2-5.
- THREE SWING SETS, WITH A TOTAL OF 10 STANDARD BELT SEATS AND FOUR MOLDED BUCKET SEATS.
- A 2,500-SQUARE-FOOT SPLASH PLAY AREA, WITH MULTIPLE WATER SPRAY JETS AND MISTING DEVICES.
- 13,000 SQUARE FEET OF RUBBERIZED BASE SURFACE TO PROTECT CHILDREN WHILE THEY'RE PLAYING.
- FOUR SHADE STRUCTURES TO KEEP PLAYGROUND USERS COOL.

Website: http://louisvilleky.gov/government/parks/park-list/iroquois-park

Adapted Leisure Activities

"Adapted Leisure Activities offers a wide range of recreational activities for individuals with mental and/or physical disabilities, along with their friends and families. Programs include wheelchair basketball, aqua exercise, bowling, dances, assisted shopping and more."

Website: http://louisvilleky.gov/government/parks/adapted-leisure-activities
Phone: 502/456.8148
Email: http://www.louisvilleky.gov/MetroParks/aboutus/contactforms/emailbjlevis.htm

Frazier Rehab Institute – Adaptive Sports Program

"The ultimate vision and goal of the Adapted Sports Program at Frazier Rehab Institute is to improve the quality of life of the individuals with disabilities and offer healthier lifestyle choices for these individuals and their families. Frazier Rehab Institute has created a greater awareness of, and generated education in, the prevention of health complications and illnesses such as: obesity, diabetes, stress and other health related concerns. These conditions are often associated with physical disabilities though the Adapted Sports Program."

Website: http://www.jhsmh.org/Health-Services/Rehab-Services-Frazier-Rehab/Specialties/Adaptive-Sports-Program.aspx
Phone: (502) 582-7618

handiCAPABLE Guide Service, Inc.

"handiCAPABLE Guide Service, Inc., is dedicated to educating and rehabilitating through recreation. We provide the developmentally delayed and physically challenged youth and adults in Kentucky and surrounding states the opportunity to experience the thrills and challenges of boating, fishing, and other forms of outdoor recreation."

Where we differ from other fishing and hunting services is that handiCAPABLE Guide service has...
- An ENTIRELY VOLUNTEER STAFF!!
- A wheelchair-accessible fishing boat with a drop-down bow and wheelchair tie downs.
- Adaptive fishing equipment available for your use during your visit.
- Volunteers trained and experienced in adaptive fishing and hunting techniques.
- Seminars on adaptive fishing and hunting that can be designed to your organization's needs, presented at your location.
- Our volunteers can travel to your location for fishing excursions, seminars, adaptive fishing equipment conversions.

Website: http://www.handicapable.net/
Email: staff@handicapable.net
Facebook: https://www.facebook.com/pages/handiCAPABLE-Guide-Service-Inc/96450521349

Center for Courageous Kids

"The Center for Courageous Kids is a place where children living with life threatening illnesses and their families could come free of charge and have fun, find respite, feel normal and forget about their everyday struggles. Our 20 million dollar funded campus encompasses an on-site medical center with helipad, indoor aquatic complex, equestrian riding arena, bowling alley, gymnasium, climbing wall, boating and fishing, theater, four camper lodges, and SO much more!"

Website: http://www.thecenterforcourageouskids.org/
Phone: 1-207-618-2900

Maryland

"Come discover what vacation is really about. A soothing sail on the Chesapeake Bay … A quiet cabin near mountain trails … A cozy clubhouse just beyond the 18thgreen … Maryland says "welcome" in so many ways.

We're passionate about giving you a complete vacation experience, so visit our five unique regions to find fishing, skiing, sightseeing, sumptuous food and sandy beaches. Pack your days with family fun – fill your nights with unforgettable entertainment." (Source: visitmaryland.org)

Baltimore Adapted Recreation and Sports

"Baltimore Adapted Recreation and Sports (BARS) is a community based, non-profit organization dedicated to providing year round recreational opportunities to both children and adults with disabilities."

Website: http://www.barsinfo.org/
Phone: 410-771-4606
Email:pam4bars@aol.com
Facebook: http://www.facebook.com/BARSMD

CRAB (Chesapeake Region Accessible Boating)

"Chesapeake Region Accessible Boating (CRAB) is a 501 (c)(3) non-profit organization dedicated to making the thrill of sailing a reality for physically and/or developmentally-challenged individuals and for those individuals whose financial circumstances preclude their participation in recreation on the waters of Chesapeake Bay."

Website: http://crabsailing.org/
Phone: (410) 626-0273
Email: info@crabsailing.org

Massachusetts

"Massachusetts has all the geographical features of the other states, from skiing and fall foliage drives in the western Berkshire Mountains to the beaches of Cape Cod and vacation islands of Martha's Vineyard and Nantucket. Boston (and its neighbor, Cambridge) is a world-class city of top-notch cultural offerings and American Revolutionary history." (source: http://www.visit-massachusetts.com/)

Piers Park Adaptive Sailing

"The Adaptive Sailing Program at Piers Park Sailing Center is a nationally recognized non-profit sailing program which has served over one thousand people with disabilities since the program's inception in 2007. In 2009, US Sailing awarded PPSC as the Best Community Program for disabled sailors. In 2010, we were honored to be designated a Paralympics Sports Club. PPSC's program objectives are to empower our sailors with disabilities to realize their recreational goals using adapted teaching methods and a full array of adapted equipment. Our sailors tell us that while learning the important sailing skills, they are rewarded with a sense o-f confidence while being challenged by the sport of sailing."

Website: http://piersparksailing.org/adaptive-sailing
Facebook: http://www.facebook.com/pierspark
Phone: 617-561-6677
Email: info@piersparksailing.org

Courageous Adaptive Sailing

These programs have produced regional, national and even world champions! At Courageous, members of these populations (mostly youth and young adults) gain a variety of physical, social, and psychological benefits, many of which are unique to the experience of sailing itself. While sailing in majestic Boston Harbor, participants build skills in teamwork, physical coordination, self-reliance, abstract thought, and leadership as well as technical knowledge of a dynamic sport.

Website: http://www.courageoussailing.org/
Facebook: https://www.facebook.com/courageoussailing
Phone: 617.242.3821

Access Sport America

Offers: windsurfing, kayaking, rowing/sculling, outrigger canoeing, water-skiing, kite sailing as well as rock/wall climbing, cycling and soccer for people with disabilities.

Website: http://www.accessportamerica.org/
Phone: 978.264.0985

All Out Adventures

All Out Adventures is a 501(c)(3) nonprofit organization whose mission is to promote health, community, and independence for people with disabilities and their family and friends through outdoor recreation. There are several programs and opportunities for people with disabilities, so check them out and join in on the fun!

Website: http://www.alloutadventures.org/

Facebook: http://www.facebook.com/pages/All-Out-Adventures/10951968427
Phone: 413.527.8980

Inclusive and Adaptive

The Adaptive Sports & Recreation Program at the Sudbury Park & Recreation Department is committed to providing year round, affordable, community based programming for individuals with disabilities. The Adaptive Sports & Recreation Program offers a comprehensive and varied program of public recreation activities, services, as well as resources for residents. Recognizing the importance of recreation and leisure in the lives of all community members, the adaptive sports and recreation programs strives to improve the quality of life for children and adults with disabilities through continued and successful involvement in sports and recreation programs.

Website: http://sudbury.ma.us/departments/Inclusive
Phone: 978-639-3257

Spaulding Rehab Network Adaptive Sports Centers

"The Spaulding Rehabilitation Network is dedicated to enabling individuals of all abilities to lead active, healthy lifestyles. Participation in sports and recreational pursuits helps to make this possible. Spaulding Adaptive Sports programs began in Boston and on Cape Cod in 2001 and in the North Shore in 2010. Since then, programming has expanded in these regions to include a broad range of land- and water-based adaptive sporting activities, all delivered with careful attention to value of sports and fitness in the rehabilitation process. Spaulding now offers adaptive sports and recreation programs from Cape Ann to Cape Cod."

Website: http://www.spauldingnetwork.org/services/inpatient/adaptive-sports.aspx

Michigan

"Michigan attractions capture our imaginations, warm our hearts, thrill us and inspire us to come back for more. Michigan's museums, water parks, wineries, zoos, lighthouses and more are ready when we are. Because discovering new delights and doing what we've always wanted to do is Pure Michigan." (Source: http://www.michigan.org/)

Camp Grace Bentley

Camp Grace Bentley hosts campers with a range of physical and mental challenges. Campers ages seven through sixteen are invited to sign up for a nine day session beginning late June and running through mid-August.

Located in Burtchville, Michigan, just north of Port Huron, a total of 11 cabins line the shore of Lake Huron, giving campers a truly rustic and authentic camping experience. Individual cabins for campers and counselors each with their own bed, closet, nightstand and private bathroom.

Website: http://www.campgracebentley.org
Facebook: http://www.facebook.com/pages/Camp-Grace-Bentley/179114562125724?v=wall
Email: campgrace@hotmail.com

Accessible Spots in Holland, Michigan

Great news! You don't have to venture across the big pond to experience old world culture; in fact, it's alive and well right here in the U.S. in places like Holland, Mich. The Dutch influence is evident throughout downtown Holland and at local spots like the Holland Museum, Windmill Island and DeKlomp Wooden Shoe and Delftware Factory.

Holland Museum

This excellent museum features a ramped side entrance and barrier-free access throughout the building. Inside this former post office, you'll find exhibits about the local history, gifts from the Netherlands, and even a display from the 1939 Golden Gate International Exposition. And don't miss the Dutch gallery, featuring 55 Dutch paintings from the 17th to 19th centuries and more than 150 cultural objects, from fine furniture and Delftware to silver and original Dutch costumes.

Source: http://www.disaboom.com/destinations/accessible-travel-in-holland-michigan-gives-a-taste-of-holland-closer-to-home
Website: http://www.hollandmuseum.org/
Facebook: http://www.facebook.com/pages/Holland-MI/Holland-Museum/117888696762?ref=s
Phone: 1 (616) 796-3329

Center for Independent Living

"We are proud of the many ways we bring meaning to our community and improve the quality of life for individuals with disabilities. Each year, we impact the lives of over 4,000 people throughout Southeast Michigan, including people with disabilities, their families and friends, and members of the business community."

Website: http://www.annarborcil.org/
Phone: (734) 971-0277
Facebook: https://www.facebook.com/AnnArborCIL

Windmill Island

For a real taste of Holland, head over to Windmill Island, a 30-acre park that boasts a miniature Dutch village, a variety of shops, and of course a windmill. Access is good throughout the park, with level access to all the shops and buildings, and wheelchair access across the flat bridge to the windmill.

The highlight of Windmill Island, the 240-year-old De Zwann windmill is America's only authentic Dutch windmill. It was carefully disassembled and shipped from Zaandam in 1965. There is level access to the bottom floor of the windmill, but the upper levels can only be accessed by stairs.

Website: http://www.cityofholland.com/windmillislandgardens
Phone: 616-355-1030
Email: windmill@cityofholland.com

Michigan Lighthouses

Michigan lighthouses are stars of the shore, beacons of brilliance and luminaries of lore. More than 115 Great Lakes lighthouses form a stellar constellation along the Michigan coastline, guiding sailors and capturing imaginations. Some still shine for ships. Others share their stories with us first-hand as museums. As bed and breakfasts and as Michigan history in the making. So let Michigan lighthouses light our way.

Frederik Meijer Gardens & Sculpture Park

"Frederik Meijer Gardens & Sculpture Park is an ADA regulated and accessible facility. Both indoor and outdoor spaces are barrier-free with ramps and paved pathways to accommodate wheelchairs and strollers and allow easy maneuverability. Courtesy wheelchairs are available for use. Although pets are prohibited, certified service dogs are welcomed with appropriate credentials."

Website: http://www.meijergardens.org/plan/accessibility/
Email: info@meijergardens.org
Facebook: https://www.facebook.com/MeijerGardens

Minnesota

"From Greyhound buses and snowmobiles to SPAM and Red Wing Pottery, Minnesota boasts a boatful of great inventions and beloved products that have been woven into American life for generations. Check out museums and factory tours devoted to the North Star state's best-known creations." (source: http://www.exploreminnesota.com/)

The Paul Bunyan Trail

The Paul Bunyan Trail is the longest paved trail in Minnesota at 112-miles and it connects the Heartland Trail, the Blue Ox Trail and the Cuyuna State Trail. The portion of the trail from Guthrie south through Laporte toward Walker is now paved. With the paving of this 19 mile segment, completed in 2010, the Paul Bunyan Trail now yields a continuously paved trail from Brainerd MN to Lake Bemidji State Park in Bemidji Minnesota–a total of 112 paved miles!
Website: http://www.paulbunyantrail.com/
Email: bigpaul@paulbunyantrail.com

United Foundation for Disabled Archers

"If you are a physically challenged hunter looking for unique bow hunting adventures, the United Foundation For Disabled Archers (UFFDA) has the opportunity you have been searching for. Each year, seasoned bow hunting volunteers sponsor free bow hunts for UFFDA's disabled members and we would consider it a privilege to entertain you on one of these hunts each year."
Website: http://www.uffdaclub.com/
Phone: 320-634-3660
Email: bowtwang@charter.net

Minnesota Adapted Athletics Association

"The goal of the program has always been to provide sports experiences for high school athletes with disabilities in the same manner that they have been provided for non-disabled athletes. The organization wanted to provide interscholastic sports opportunities where none previously existed. This has been achieved in the state of Minnesota. Minnesota is the first state where adapted sports have been officially sanctioned by a state high school league. The following indoor sports are offered by the MSHSL: Adapted Soccer (Fall), Adapted Floor Hockey (Winter), Adapted Softball (Spring) and Adapted Bowling (Spring)."

Website: http://www.mnadaptedathletics.org
Phone: 651-324-0420
Email: maaasecretary@izoom.net

The Courage Center

"Courage Center is a Minnesota-based, nonprofit rehabilitation and resource center that serves children and adults experiencing barriers to health and independence. Courage Center specializes in treating brain injury, spinal cord injury, stroke, chronic pain, autism, and disabilities experienced since birth. Founded in 1928, Courage Center offers advanced technologies and innovation provided in part through the efforts of thousands of volunteers and donors."

Website: http://www.allinahealth.org/Courage-Kenny-Rehabilitation-Institute/
Phone: 763-588-0811

Mississippi

"Visit Mississippi and find out what real Southern hospitality feels like. Whether you're seeking blues music, craft beer, civil rights, country music, tamales, civil war history, or seafood, Mississippi has a trail for that." (source: http://www.visitmississippi.org/)

Steamboat Natchez

"The New Orleans Steamboat Company locally owns and operates the last authentic Steamboat on the Mighty Mississippi River. The Steamboat NATCHEZ Dinner Jazz and Daytime jazz cruises run daily, year round, in the style of authentic steamboats in New Orleans for centuries! The boat is wheelchair accessible."

Website: http://www.steamboatnatchez.com/
Phone: (504) 569-1401
Email: cruises@neworleanssteamboat.com
Facebook: http://www.facebook.com/SteamboatNatchez

Disability Connection Community Playground

The Bruce Ladner Memorial Park is being upgraded to a fully accessible playground that can be enjoyed by everyone with special consideration of children and adults with disabilities. The park has bathrooms, shade, and a walking track. Phase 1 opened on May 4, 2012.

Website: http://www.co.harrison.ms.us/departments/parks/

Missouri

"With over 120 wineries across the state, baseball, boating adventures and scenic river ways, Missouri is the perfect destination for a weekend getaway." (source: http://www.visitmo.com/)

Camp Barnabas

We offer acceptance and love to more than 1,500 campers with special needs and chronic diseases – and their siblings – in locations across the United States. Through adaptive activities, people with physical, intellectual, and/or medical challenges become participants, not observers, in the world around them. They leave Camp Barnabas knowing they are uniquely created to live lives of ability.

Website: http://www.campbarnabas.org/
Email: info@campbarnabas.org
Phone: 417.476.2565
Facebook: http://www.facebook.com/campbarnabas

Wonderland Camp

Wonderland Camp provides a fun, educational camp experience for mentally and physically individuals, to offer a respite from daily care giving for family members and health care workers and to provide and nurture a personal development experience for volunteers and staff. Wonderland Camp now has the 1st Wheelchair Accessible Treehouse in Missouri.

Website: www.wonderlandcamp.org
Email: Info@wonderlandcamp.org
Phone: 573-392-1000

Accessible Arts

To unlock the arts for children with disabilities and advocate access to the arts. The arts invite people to leave familiar territory, to explore new answers and seek new questions. The arts offer a means to self-expression, communication, and independence. By learning through the arts, students become lifelong learners, experiencing the joy of discovery and exploration, and the value of each other's ideas.

Website: http://www.accessiblearts.org/
Phone: 913.281.1133
Facebook: http://www.facebook.com/pages/Accessible-ArtsVSA-Kansas-Inc/257212576879?ref=ts

Meramec Caverns

"Beneath the fertile rolling hills of the Meramec Valley, lies a complex of mineral formations and color as rare and unique as they are beautiful. These jewels of nature which took thousands of years to grow, are preserved in the spectacular sights of Meramec Caverns.

Guided tours by trained rangers are conducted along well-lighted walkways. All cavern facilities are accessible to the disabled. Learn how an ancient limestone "Wine Table" and an entire 7-story mansion were built... all underground. On tour you will see both the rarest and largest cave formations in the world.

Meramec Caverns is wheelchair accessible. Of the 80 minute tour, the first 50 minutes covers flat terrain with the last 30 minutes containing one flight of stairs. Stairs can easily be by-passed through use of a nearby ramp, but requires the assistance of a physically fit person."

Website: www.americascave.com
Email: info@americascave.com
Phone: 573-468-CAVE (2283)

Nevada

"Make Nevada your summertime destination! Choose from scenic wonders like stunning Lake Tahoe and the incredible Hoover Dam. Nevada's diverse regions offer visitors an abundance of activities.

With abundant outdoor recreation, unique attractions, exciting events, world-class shows, and special exhibits, there's no shortage of things to do in Nevada. You just might have to extend your vacation." (Source: travelnevada.com)

Las Vegas Accessibility

"Vegas is a service-oriented town dedicated to making vacations comfortable and enjoyable for everyone regardless of their physical abilities. We've put together some helpful tips and information on getting around the city for those visitors with special needs."

Website: http://www.vegas.com/lounge/handicapped.html

Wheelchair Getaways

"Wheelchair Getaways of Las Vegas, Nevada provides quality accessible van rentals throughout the Las Vegas Area. All of our vehicles are wheelchair accessible, with lowered floors and automatic ramps. Many of our wheelchair accessible van rental customers want to travel to the Grand Canyon, no problem – a great adventure. Hoover Dam is on the way and highly accessible.

Whether you are going through rehabilitation, replacing a vehicle that has been in an accident, or are simply traveling to the great state of Nevada, Wheelchair Getaways of Las Vegas has your transportation solution. Our rental vans are available by the day, week, month, or longer, insuring that you have 24-hour transportation for all your needs."

Website: http://www.wheelchairgetaways.com/franchise/nevada_lasvegas/home.htm
Phone: 1-800-642-2042
Email: info@wheelchairgetaways.com

Turning Point Nation

"Turning Point was founded in 1979 by Michael "Shorty" Powers. After an injury at age 17 left Shorty without the use of his legs he began looking for opportunities to become involved in the outdoor recreational activities that he had always loved. He found no organized activities that were available to people who had major mobility impairments. Not willing to give up his love of fishing, kayaking, scuba diving and hunting, Shorty established Turning Point to assure that outdoor activities were readily available to people with many types of physical challenges. Turning Point is a 501(c) 3 nonprofit organization designed to teach people with mobility impairments the skills necessary to fully enjoy the outdoors, and to provide free or low cost activities. Turning Point provides the encouragement and support needed for people who have major physical challenges in life to fully participate in the adventure of living."

Website: http://www.turningpointnation.org/

Phone: 530-414-4804
Email: ccable@turningpointnation.org

New Jersey

"New Jersey has destinations and attractions that draw millions of visitors each year. One example is the fabled Jersey Shore that's a magnet for families and individuals who seek the sun, surf, water activities and the excitement and fun of the state's boardwalks.

All around the state visitors will find fabulous shopping and there are hundreds of festivals and other special events that can be found year round." (source: http://www.visitnj.org/)

Tri-State Wheelchair and Ambulatory Athletics

"The Tri-State Wheelchair Athletic Association (TSWAA) is dedicated to foster disabled individual independence through Sport. Chartered to operate in the Connecticut, New York and New Jersey areas, TSWAA offers a structure for disabled teams and individuals to compete in multiple sports.

Tri-States offers disabled athletes the opportunity to participate in multiple sport opportunities in many sports."

Website: http://www.tswaa.com/
Facebook: http://www.facebook.com/tswaa1
Phone: 201-435-1688

Edgemont Park All Children's Playground

This playground is available for children of all ages AND abilities! It is one of the biggest playgrounds in the area. It has a rubber ground, so kids in wheelchairs are able to transport easily. It is safe, has plenty of slides and is fun!

Website: http://www.njplaygrounds.com/732/edgemont-memorial-park-montclair-nj/

Memorial Park

A group of Boy Scouts founded this accessible playground which contains several ramps and a rubber ground that is convenient for kids in wheelchairs. There are even four special needs swings and accessible picnic benches.

Website: http://www.njplaygrounds.com/746/memorial-park-westfield-nj/

Phil Rizzuto Park

"The County of Union also recently opened Phil Rizzuto Park on the borders of Elizabeth/Union/Hillside in honor of the New York Yankee Hall-of-Fame baseball player who lives nearby. The park is a 10.4-acre multi-use facility that also contains a "Boundless Playground" area, which allows children with disabilities to play alongside their peers."

website: http://www.njplaygrounds.com/250/phil-rizzuto-park-union-nj/

Avalon

"If you are looking for adventure, there are unlimited activities to keep you busy. For the water lovers, you can enjoy boating, sailing, wave running, kayaking, paddle boarding, water skiing, wakeboarding, fishing, surfing and swimming in our ocean and back bays. If staying on land suits you better, take up a game of beach volleyball, play tennis at one of our newly renovated courts, or visit one of our nine parks and playgrounds."

Website: http://www.visitavalonnj.com/beach
Facebook: https://www.facebook.com/avalonnewjersey

Operation Beachhead

"The mission of Operation Beachhead is to offer veterans, troops, disabled individuals and their families, adaptive recreational, sports and social activities."

Website: http://www.opbeachhead.org/
Email: opbeachhead@gmail.com
Facebook: https://www.facebook.com/operationbeachhead?fref=ts

New York

"Trek through the high peaks of the Adirondacks, rent a rustic cabin in the Catskills, taste the famous ice wines of the Finger Lakes Region, or head to Coney Island and ride the oldest wooden roller coaster in the United States. There is so much more to New York than New York. (source: http://www.iloveny.com/)

The Metropolitan Museum of Art

"The Museum is committed to making its collection, buildings, programs, and services accessible to all audiences. We offer programs for visitors with disabilities on a regular basis. No matter who you are or what your age, there are so many wonderful ways to learn about art and the Met's collection, both online and at the Museum. Explore programs and resources that introduce you to new worlds or offer more about familiar territory. The Met has something for everyone!"

Website: http://www.metmuseum.org/visit/accessibility
Email: education@metmuseum.org
Facebook: https://www.facebook.com/metmuseum

Helen Hayes Adapted Sports

"From sailing to cycling and golf to gardening, the HHH Adapted Sports & Recreation Program is a four-season initiative serving individuals with a range of abilities, interests and skills. Leisure opportunities are an important component of an active and healthy lifestyle, fostering rehabilitation, recovery and camaraderie, and the Adapted Sports & Rec Program is dedicated to offering a range of recreational and competitive events. The program reaches out to current and former patients, as well as individuals living in the community who may be interested in trying out a new activity or resuming a sport or activity they may have enjoyed prior to acquiring a disability. Prior experience is not required to participate in any activity."

Website: http://helenhayeshospital.org/adapted-sports-recreation/
Phone: 845-786-4000
Facebook: https://www.facebook.com/pages/Helen-Hayes-Hospital/170913566301293 New York

Adaptive Sports Foundation

"ASF students are five years of age and older and live with disabilities ranging from relatively mild learning disabilities to more severe disabilities such as paralysis, autism, amputation, cerebral palsy and traumatic brain injury. Founded in 1984, the Foundation's work promotes physical activity for children and adults with disabilities by offering winter programs for recreational skiing, snowboarding, snowshoeing, yoga and personal fitness.

Additionally, the ASF supports a competitive race team for athletes with both physical and cognitive challenges, as well as a 12-week residential competition program for Paralympics eligible athletes.

The ASF Summer Program includes paddling, windsurfing, fly fishing, cycling, fitness training, yoga, golf and waterskiing."

Website: http://www.adaptivesportsfoundation.org/
Phone: (518) 734-5070
Email: asfwindham@mhcable.com
Facebook: http://www.facebook.com/asfwindham

Y-Knot Sailing

"Participation in a sport like sailing builds confidence and self-esteem, while it challenges the whole person. Y-Knot is all about sailing — regardless of your experience or physical abilities. If you're someone with a disability looking for a new challenge, or an able-bodied sailor interested in seeing your sport in a completely new light, contact us. We'll be happy to share our dream with you and demonstrate how sailing lets us "leave our disabilities on the shore.""

Website: http://www.yknotsailing.org/
Phone: (518) 656-9462

Accessible Niagara

"Getting out and about is important. It helps keep us sane. Whether you live in Niagara or want to visit as a tourist, if you're mobility impaired, this site will help you choose your accessible destinations."

Website: http://www.accessibleniagara.com/

Mid Hudson Valley Camp

The Mid-Hudson Valley Camp is an American Camp Association certified summer camp that serves a diverse group of people. What started as a one-week summer session for children with disabilities in the 1970s has blossomed into a nine-week camp program that caters to the needs of children and adults with developmental, mental, and physical disabilities, deaf children, children living with cancer, pediatric patients from Harlem Hospital's Family Care Center, and inner-city students. For over 35 years, the camp has served hundreds of persons with disabilities and continues to provide children, teens, and adults with a joy-filled summer camp experience.

Website: http://esopuscamps.com/

Lawrence gets out and enjoys life in New York City. Photo courtesy of Get Out, Enjoy Life campaign.

Accessible NYC

"Our goal is to establish a coalition of public and private partners dedicated to serving the disability community that can be comprised of businesses committed to serving travelers with disabilities.

To create an informed and thorough process and infrastructure, Accessible NYC plans to engage at least the following groups of stakeholder partners to achieve its goals, namely public agencies & their constituencies, non-profits who serve the disability community, the disability community itself, and the businesses and providers who serve the disability community."

Website: http://accessiblenyc.org/
Phone: 718-507-0500
Email: edkelley@accessiblenyc.com

Ohio

"From adventure-filled days to dazzling nightlife, Ohio has something for everyone. Let us entertain, enrich and inspire you with our world-class museums, quaint galleries, vibrant performing arts and museums.

Or, if sports are more of interest to you, play ball, go swimming, golfing, hiking, birding, canoeing, camping or whatever your sport. So many choices make Ohio a fabulous place to visit." (source: http://consumer.discoverohio.com/default.aspx)

Ohio Wheelchair Sports Association

Welcome to OWSA, a wheelchair sports association consisting of several wheelchair sports teams based in Columbus, Ohio. The Ohio Wheelchair Sports Association is a non-profit 501(c)3 organization relying on the fund raising initiatives of its members as well as donations of Columbus businesses.

The mission is to encourage and promote the nurturing and development of individual and team adaptive competitive and recreational sports in the State of Ohio.

Website: http://ohwcsports.webs.com/
Facebook: https://www.facebook.com/OHWCSports
Phone: 614.915.2865
Email: mschreiber@ohwcsports.org

Adaptive Sports Program of Ohio

ASPO's has two Quad Rugby teams. For current practice dates and times please visit their website. The Adaptive Sports Program of Ohio (ASPO) is a 501(c)3 organization established to promote the health and wellness of individuals with physical disabilities by providing competitive and recreational adaptive sport opportunities throughout the State of Ohio. Currently, ASPO offers eight sports in Northeast Ohio, and has partnered with the U.S. Olympic Committee to offer Paralympics Sport Northeast Ohio. Our headquarters are in Wooster, Ohio, however, we have active programming in Cleveland, Akron, Columbus, Wooster, and more!

Video: http://www.youtube.com/watch?feature=player_embedded&v=7CXCWVk7ZXU
Website: http://adaptivesportsohio.org/sports/wheelchair-rugby
Phone: 330-262-1200
Facebook: http://www.facebook.com/pages/Adaptive-Sports-Program-of-Ohio/226960990268

Access Travel Center – State Wide Delivery in Ohio

AccessTravelCenter.com has the World's Best Single Source of Valuable Travel and Health Information for people with special needs. There are multiple locations throughout Ohio. It is simple to make a reservation—online or over the phone!

Website: http://www.accesstravelcenter.com/abvanoh.html
Phone: 1-800-584-7368

Ohio Handcycle Network

The Ohio Handcycle Network rides with all levels of experience. We always welcome new riders and new places to ride. There are no membership fees, no one who is considered in charge. It is just a group of friends who share the same passion for riding, and who enjoy allowing others to try this healthy experience. We also work with several places that rent Handcycles so that anyone can enjoy a ride.

Website: http://www.ohiowheelchair.com/OhioHandcycleGroup.htm
Email: OhioWheelchair@gmail.com

Buckeye Wellness Center – Spinal Cord Fitness

The BWC combines technology and exercise to maximize recovery and provide
enhanced quality of life for people living with spinal cord injuries. It was founded by a C5/C6 quadriplegic.

Website: http://www.buckeyewellnesscenter.com/Home_Page.html
Facebook: https://www.facebook.com/buckeyewellnesscenter
Phone: (216) 816 6860

Three Trackers of Ohio

Three Trackers of Ohio is a volunteer non-profit organization dedicated to the promotion of adaptive recreational sports to persons with or without physical disabilities. The organization began over 35 years ago when several people with amputated legs decided they wanted to share their passion for downhill skiing. In addition to snow skiing, Three Trackers also has an adaptive water ski program and holds an annual white water rafting trip.

Website: http://3trackers.org/index.html
Email: md1053@aol.com
Facebook: https://www.facebook.com/3trackersofohio

Oklahoma

"Whether planning a family vacation, a road trip with friends, or a romantic getaway for two, you'll find that Oklahoma is home to an amazing variety of attractions and activities. Get a sense of the natural allure of Oklahoma by visiting one of our 34 state parks. In addition to relaxing in the beautiful surroundings - lakes, mountains, sand dunes, and forests - you can hike, bike, fish or participate in organized park activities. Then rest in a comfortable lodge or cabin, or camp in your own tent or RV.

Find the perfect outdoor adventure to get you off the couch and into the great outdoors at any of the 34 diverse Oklahoma State Parks. Go rappelling at Red Rock Canyon State Park or boulder hopping and climbing at Robbers Cave State Park. Bring your own dune buggy or rent an ATV and fly over the dunes at Little Sahara State Park or grab your wet suit and have a scuba adventure in Lake Tenkiller's dive park." (source: http://www.travelok.com/)

Boathouse District

"Join us on the water and experience the thrill of kayaking on the Oklahoma River! This free program introduces adults ages 18+ with physical and visual disabilities (and their caregivers) to the sport of canoe/kayak. No experience is necessary; we'll show you everything you need to know and provide all equipment to ensure you have a safe, fun time on the water."

"Recreational kayaks can be outfitted to meet individual needs with pontoons available to provide extra stability when needed. Paddle adaptations are also available for those with grip limitations, and trunk support is available for those with limited mobility."

Website: http://boathousedistrict.org/adaptive-kayaking/
Email: asaleh@okcbf.org,
Facebook: https://www.facebook.com/OKCBoathouseDistrict?_rdr

National Cowboy Hall of Fame and Western Heritage

"The National Cowboy Western & Heritage Museum is America's premier institution of Western history, art and culture. Founded in 1955, the museum in Oklahoma City collects, preserves and exhibits an internationally renowned collection of Western art and artifacts while sponsoring dynamic educational programs to stimulate interest in the enduring legacy of our American West. More than 10 million visitors from around the world have sought out this unique museum to gain better understanding of the West: a region and a history that permeates our national culture."

Website: http://nationalcowboymuseum.org/
Email: sstrain@nationalcowboymuseum.org
Facebook: https://www.facebook.com/ncwhm

Oklahoma City National Memorial and Museum

"The Memorial Museum is an interactive learning experience that takes you on a chronological self-guided tour through the story of April 19, 1995, and the days, weeks and years that followed the bombing of Oklahoma City's Alfred P. Murrah Federal Building. The story tracks the remarkable journey of loss, resilience, justice and hope."

Website: https://oklahomacitynationalmemorial.org/
Phone: 405.235.3313
Facebook: https://www.facebook.com/okcmemorial

Oklahoma WONDERtorium

"At the Oklahoma WONDERtorium we believe in inspiring curiosity to learn through play... for a lifetime. Every day, our expertly designed exhibits and programs open doors for Oklahoma's curious young minds to express what they know and to discover, create and explore more – on their own terms."

"Designed primarily for children ages 12 and younger, the Oklahoma WONDERtorium is recognized regionally as a cultural and educational institution serving children and families onsite and through outreach programs. The Museum's exhibits and innovative educational programs emphasize hands-on engagement and learning through experience, employing play as a tool to spark the inherent creativity, curiosity, and imagination of children. Exhibits explore science, math, creativity, history, culture, health & wellness, dramatic play and the problem-solving."

Website: https://www.okwondertorium.org/
Phone: (405) 533-3333
Facebook: https://www.facebook.com/okwondertorium

National Weather Center

"The National Weather Center houses a unique confederation of University of Oklahoma, National Oceanic and Atmospheric Administration and state organizations that work together in partnership to improve understanding of events occurring in Earth's atmosphere over a wide range of time and space."

Website: http://www.ou.edu/content/nwc.html
Email: info@nwcnorman.org
Facebook: https://www.facebook.com/nwcnorman.org

Oregon

"Oregon isn't a place you see as much as you do. You can sight-see our beautiful coast, volcanic mountains, crystal-clear lakes and deserts that stretch as far as the eye can see. If you're looking for world-class pinots, some of the best food and craft beer in the country, epic cycling, kayaking, windsurfing or just about anything else-ing, look no further. Better yet, don't look, come out here and leap." (Source: Traveloregon.com)

Camp Attitude

In 1998, Camp Attitude was nothing more than a dream. The property was covered with overgrown brush and unkempt trees and didn't seem to have much potential for anything, let alone a place where people with special needs could attend summer camp and explore the great outdoors. Thankfully, there was a group of people that could vision a fully accessible campground with full amenities. It seemed at the time to be a herculean task because it would require countless hours of volunteer work, donations of material, and intense fund raising.

In 2000, Camp Attitude became a reality. The campus included; three full cabins, fully accessible bathing facilities, two story staff house, multipurpose room, industrial kitchen, over 2 miles of paved trails, fishing pond, and more.

Today, many of the facilities have been upgraded and Camp Attitude has become a premiere campground. We welcome you to look around our website, contact us directly with questions, or visit our facilities in person.

Website: http://www.campattitude.com/
Phone: 541.367.3420
Email: campinfo@campattitude.com
Facebook: http://www.facebook.com/campattitude

Oregon Disability Sports

Oregon Disability Sports is a non-profit organization that empowers people with physical disabilities through sport and fitness. We serve as a resource for healthy physical activities for the physically disabled by providing support for competitive athletes striving for excellence and by promoting general fitness and providing outlets for recreation and competition. The purpose of those athletic opportunities is to teach and develop life skills (self confidence, socialization, independence, etc.) to people so that they can better participate in society.
Website: http://www.oregondisabilitysports.net/
Phone: 503-241-0850
Email: trisha@oregondisabilitysports.net
Facebook: http://www.facebook.com/pages/Oregon-Disability-Sports/113301762020665

Chehalem Mountain Therapy Riding Center

The mission of CMTRCI is to improve the lives of persons with special needs through the interaction with horses while fostering a safe, life enhancing, mentally and physically enriching, rewarding experience. Networking community, government, health professionals, and researchers, CMTRCI encourages a team approach of working together to change lives.

Website: http://www.horsebacktherapy.com/index.html

Email: director@horsebacktherapy.com

Adaptive and Inclusive Recreation (AIR)

"Offering community-based recreation activities and leisure services specially designed for children, teens, and adults who have a disability and/or special needs. Our services are designed to assist people in developing and using their leisure time in ways that enhance their health, well-being, and independence."

Website: http://www.portlandonline.com/parks/index.cfm?c=39830
Phone: 503-823-4328
Email: kevin.mattias@portlandoregon.gov

Pennsylvania

"No matter where in America you call home, there is a part of Pennsylvania that is yours forever – our heritage. From Independence Hall in Philadelphia, to the battlefield at Gettysburg. From the Horseshoe Curve near Altoona, to the Underground Railroad on our side of the Mason-Dixon line. From the coal miners' village of Eckely, to the recreated cities of Pittsburgh and Bethlehem. In all of these places and many more, your heritage is preserved, revealed, recreated, and waiting for you to discover.

This history gave rise to charming towns, Amish villages, Victorian manors, ornate theaters, historic architecture, and world-renowned museums. Today, as always, the arts bring every corner of Pennsylvania to life – in vibrant concert venues and countless arts festivals in downtowns and countrysides. " (Source: Tom Corbett, Governor of Pennsylvania)

Freedom's Wings

"Freedom's Wings International (FWI) is a non-profit organization run by and for people with physical disabilities. We provide the opportunity for those who are physically challenged to fly in specially adapted sailplanes, either as a passenger or as a member of the flight training program.

The purpose of Freedom's Wings International is to bring the world of soaring to disabled persons by:

- EXPOSING PERSONS WITH DISABILITIES TO THE SOARING EXPERIENCE
- TEACHING QUALIFIED PERSONS WITH DISABILITIES TO SOAR
- PROVIDING FACILITIES FOR SOARING TO THOSE PERSONS WITH DISABILITIES ABLE TO SOAR
- PROVIDING TRAINING FOR INSTRUCTORS, GROUND CREW, AND FLYING STUDENTS
- PROVIDING A NON-PROFIT EDUCATIONAL AND FRATERNAL ORGANIZATION
- SERVING AS A RESOURCE AND MODEL FOR OTHER ORGANIZATIONS WITH SIMILAR INTENT

FWI works closely with local and national organizations for people with physical disabilities and encourages organizations to learn more about our programs."

Website: http://freedomswings.org/
Phone: (800) 382-1197
Email: rrfucci@earthlink.net

American Dance Wheels

American Dance Wheels is an artistic organization that trains individuals with disabilities, their able-bodied partners, ballroom dance teachers, adaptive recreational therapists as well as occupational and physical therapists the art of Wheelchair Ballroom and Latin Dancing. Seminars for individuals, professional dance teachers and therapists are held so that this method of wheelchair dancing can be taught to people using wheelchairs in all communities.

Website: http://www.americandancewheels.com/
Phone: 215-588-6671

Facebook: http://www.facebook.com/pages/American-DanceWheels-Foundation/57815487088

Three Rivers Adaptive Sports

To promote quality of life, education and to provide quality year-round sports and recreation opportunities for people with disabilities, their families and friends.

Website: http://www.traspa.org
Phone: 412-848-8896
Email: MARK4TRAS@COMCAST.NET
Facebook: http://www.facebook.com/pages/Three-Rivers-Adaptive-Sports/274619025273

Gettysburg National Military Park

The Battle of Gettysburg was a turning point in the Civil War, the Union victory that ended General Robert E. Lee's second and most ambitious invasion of the North. Often referred to as the "High Water Mark of the Rebellion", Gettysburg was the war's bloodiest battle with 51,000 casualties. It was also the inspiration for President Abraham Lincoln's immortal "Gettysburg Address"

The park has more than 26 miles of paved roads open for touring by private vehicle. Visitors with special needs may tour the park on their own with the use of the Official Map and Guide that includes a map of the park and self-guiding auto tour, or with a licensed battlefield guide (recommended), both of which are available at the National Park Service Museum and Visitor Center at 1195 Baltimore Pike, Gettysburg. Access to exhibits at tour stops are designed to be mobility friendly and accessible though uneven surfaces and weather may affect access. If this condition is found, the park would appreciate a call from the affected party so the situation can be remedied.

Website: http://www.nps.gov/gett/index.htm

Woodlands

"The Woodlands is a non-profit organization dedicated to enriching the lives of children and adults with disability and chronic illness. Using its fully accessible and barrier-free facilities, the Woodlands' programs enable participants to experience social, cultural, environmental, recreational and spiritual growth. Serenely nestled in the North Hills of Pittsburgh, the Woodlands' 52-acre site features: an indoor heated pool, 48-bed lodge, dining hall, creative arts and computer lab, activity center, camping area, sports court, nature trail, adapted zip line, amphitheater, adapted kitchen, adapted archery range, and a par-3 adapted golf course."

Website: http://mywoodlands.org/
Email: lmortimer@woodlandsfoundation.org
Facebook: https://www.facebook.com/WoodlandsFoundation

Presque Isle

"It's never hard to find something to do at Presque Isle State Park. Add in all the organized activities on the agenda and you'll need to make some choices about how to spend your time at the park. There is also a list of accessible beaches and beach wheelchairs available"

Website: http://www.presqueisle.org/things-to-do/beaches/
Email: presqueislesp@pa.gov

Facebook: https://www.facebook.com/pages/Presque-Isle-State-Park-PA/153596731342335

Indian Valley Scuba

"Indian Valley Scuba is Philadelphia area's leading source for scuba training, exotic travel adventures, quality diving equipment, and premium gear service for water sports enthusiasts of all ages. Our convenient location in Harleysville, PA, is within a few hours' drive of major metropolitan areas including New York, Connecticut, New Jersey, Maryland, Virginia, Delaware & Pennsylvania. Ranked by the Professional Association of Dive Instructors (PADI) as the #1 dive training center in the Northeast United States, IVS offers over 30 years of diving, travel and teaching experience to ensure an extraordinary level of deliberately different scuba training and diving opportunities, from "Learn to Dive" to preparing for a career as a scuba instructor."

Website: http://www.indianvalleyscuba.com/
Email: Info@indianvalleyscuba.com
Facebook: https://www.facebook.com/indianvalleyscuba

Rhode Island

"Rhode Island, the Ocean State, is loved for its many beaches, for the historic city of Newport, and for the up-and-coming capital city of Providence, rich with culture and interesting dining. Visitors love the unspoiled Block Island, easily reached by ferry from the fishing village of Point Judith. Other parts of the state are rich in history, farms, and beautiful outdoor getaways." (source: http://www.visitri.com/state/)

Sail to Prevail (Newport, RI

"Operating in several states, Sail To Prevail teaches over 1,500 people with disability the skills of sailing in our fleet of specially adapted sailboats each year. The Sail To Prevail fleet includes five 20-foot "Freedom" sailboats, 23-foot "Sonars," a "Martin 16," and most unique, "EASTERNER" a 66-foot, handicap-accessible, America's Cup racing boat – the only one of its kind. Our programs strongly encourage disabled individuals to be active participants, steering the boat as well as opportunities to grind winches and trim sails. The measurable outcomes demonstrate self-confidence, leadership and teamwork. First time and experienced sailors are welcome at Sail To Prevail. Our program is available to all people with disabilities and has programs designed to meet specific needs."

Website: www.sailtoprevail.org
Phone: 401-849-8898
Facebook: http://www.facebook.com/pages/Sail-To-Prevail-The-National-Disabled-Sailing-Program/187998341211044

USA Wheelchair Basketball – Women's National Team

"The National Wheelchair Basketball Association (NWBA) is comprised of over 200 wheelchair basketball teams across twenty-two conferences and seven divisions. The NWBA was founded in 1948, and today consists of seven divisions including: Championship Division, Division III, Women's Division, Intercollegiate Men's Division and Intercollegiate Women's Division, as well a Junior 10' and Junior Prep Divisions."

"The National Wheelchair Basketball Association hosts the NWBA National Tournament each year where the top teams from each division come together to compete for their national title."

Website: http://www.nwba.org/
Email: info@nwba.org
Facebook: https://www.facebook.com/UsaWheelchairBasketballWomensNationalTeam?fref=ts

South Carolina

"From Table Rock in the foothills of the Blue Ridge Mountains to the wide sandy beaches of our breathtaking coastline, the Palmetto State is made for vacation. From the crystal clear water of Lake Jocassee to the cobblestone streets of historic Charleston. From delicacies like she-crab soup to more South Carolina events and festivals than there are days of the year to 368 emerald green golf courses and 47 unique and beautiful South Carolina state parks. From our quaint small towns to our Heritage Corridor to incredible shopping, entertainment and nightlife… if vacation is on your mind, it's time you put South Carolina vacations on your calendar." (Source: www.discoversouthcarolina.com)

Anchors Away

"Since 1995, the program has worked to do away with the 'anchors' that have traditionally limited people with disabilities, youth at risk and the elderly in the South Carolina area. Anchors Away serves all types of abilities and gender/age/race populations and defines a person with a disability as anyone who does not have equal access or ability to utilize the same recreational resources that are available to the majority of the community.

Anchors Away has made progress towards eliminating our community's practice of excluding individuals with disabilities and the elderly from participating in physical activities."

Website: http://anchorsawayprogram.org
Phone: 843.792.0721
Email: dave@anchorsawayprogram.org

Achieving Wheelchair Equality (North Charleston)

"Achieving Wheelchair Equality (AWE) was founded in 1991 to help wheelchair users and others with mobility problems overcome the unique obstacles they face with employment, community, family, and recreation. Our members are involved with volunteer efforts throughout the lowcountry to meet that goal. AWE encourages community involvement at all levels. But we are not known as an "All work and no play" type of organization. We sponsor several lowcountry athletes in sports such as wheelchair racing and weightlifting, and we sponsor the North Charleston Hurricanes, our local Wheelchair Basketball team. We added "Lowcountry Wheelchair Sports" to our name to reflect the demand and emphasis for recreational activities for those with disabilities."

Website: http://www.knology.net/~drc/awe/
Phone: (843) 225-5080
Email: awelcws@aol.com

Heroes on Horseback

"Heroes on Horseback is a non-profit, premier accredited operating center of PATH, Intl. (Professional Association of Therapeutic Horsemanship International) that fosters safe, professional and ethical equine assisted activities for individuals in the Lowcountry with physical, mental or emotional disabilities without regard to race, color, and creed."

Website: http://heroesonhorseback.org/

Phone: 843.757.5607
Email: info@heroesonhorseback.org

Myrtle Beach

Myrtle Beach is an accessible beach destination. They offer free beach wheelchairs, free parking, and dozens of accessible beach entries.

Website: http://www.cityofmyrtlebeach.com/handicapped.html
Phone: 843.918.1382
Email: info@cityofmyrtlebeach.com

National Park Service

"Congaree National Park offers all visitors the opportunity to recreate and enjoy the solitude of wilderness. No roads travel through the park, and all activities require a certain amount of walking. While the majority of the park is unimproved, the area around the Harry Hampton Visitor Center is accessible to all visitors so that they are able to experience one of the last great old-growth forests in the country."

Website: http://www.nps.gov/cong/planyourvisit/accessibility.htm
Phone: 803-776-4396
Facebook: https://www.facebook.com/nationalparkservice

Tennessee

"Traveling to Tennessee makes sense. We have natural beauty, southern hospitality, serene weather, and something for everyone. And, we are within a day's drive of 65 percent of the United States population. What more could you want in a travel destination? Tennessee welcomes you to explore everything we have to offer." (source: TNvacation.com)

Ashley Nicole Dream Playground

"The experiences of a little girl named Ashley Nicole Manes and her younger sister, Allison, are the inspiration to build a universally accessible playground in Knoxville. Ashley and Allison were involved in a fatal car accident with their mother in Powell in 1999. Ashley, who was four years old at the time, received the most severe injuries in the accident, even though she was properly restrained. Her neck was broken; and now, she is paralyzed from her neck down.

After a long stay in the hospital and rehabilitation centers, Ashley is back home with her parents and 3 year-old sister, Allison. The whole family is learning to live differently than they had ever imagined. Many things have changed for them. The most important things have not changed though. For instance, before the car accident, Ashley was a fun-loving, bright, playful, particularly bold, and precocious little girl, and she still very much is. Ashley's body changed dramatically, but her essence has not changed. And since returning home from the hospital, the family has resumed their life. Ashley's parents have taken her to church, to the Children's Rehabilitation Center, to parties and cookouts with friends, to the zoo and to community playgrounds with her little sister. Remarkably, of all these places, the playgrounds are the least fun for Ashley, because she cannot participate."

Website: http://www.cityofknoxville.org/parks/ashleynicole.asp
Email: allplay@dreamplayground.org

Able Youth

"I started this program as a vehicle to introduce children in wheelchairs to the world of competitive wheelchair sports. I soon realized that not all kids shared my same passion for sports. I knew the mission had to change: not every child in a wheelchair needs to shoot three pointers, or hit topspin forehands, or ski like an Olympian, but all kids in wheelchairs do need to learn."

Website: http://www.ableyouth.org
Facebook: http://www.facebook.com/home.php#!/groups/ableyouth/

Accessible Parks

The Tennessee Department of Environment and Conservation and Tennessee State Parks have worked diligently to provide reasonable accommodations to its patrons with disabilities to provide opportunities for persons with disabilities to participate in the outdoor programs and activities. Tennessee State Parks has been very sensitive in ensuring that all new construction and existing facilities provide reasonable accommodations for inclusiveness in accordance with the Americans with Disabilities Act (ADA). This effort is directed towards, employment, providing accessible inn rooms, dining areas, camp grounds, bath houses, visitors' centers, overlooks, fishing piers, boat docks, golf courses, cabins, shelters, swimming pools, trails, exhibit areas and some natural areas.

Website: http://www.tennessee.gov/environment/parks/accessguide.shtml

Sports Abilities

Sports Abilities is the premier resource for people with disabilities to find recreational, advocacy, support, and sporting activities in the nation.   We have calendars for every state and 27 different activities ranging from Basketball and Rock Climbing to Fundraisers and Social Gatherings. We believe that having one online location for people to visit to see all that is happening will help increase program participation, promote awareness, and help improve people's lives.

Website: http://www.sportsabilities.com/index.php?id=88
Facebook: https://www.facebook.com/SportsAbilities

Texas

"Stroll down warm, sandy beaches along the coast. Explore majestic canyons and forests. Play cowboy and relive history at The Alamo. Enjoy world-famous art, music and food. Shop for one-of-a-kind treasures. No matter what kind of adventure you're looking for, you'll find it in Texas." (source: http://www.discoveramerica.com/usa/states/texas.aspx)

Morgan's Wonderland

This magical amusement park is available for all ages and all special needs. It is safe, clean and fully accessible. There are several accessible rides, attractions, shows, playscapes, activities, and more! The park welcomes service animals as well and provides shady rest areas for them and the guests. This is the first ever Ultra-Accessible Family Fun Park in the world, stretching across 25 acres of San Antonio's northeast side.

Website: http://www.morganswonderland.com/
Facebook: http://www.facebook.com/MorgansWonderland
Phone: 210-495-5888

Houston Parks and Recreation Department MMSC Adaptive Sports and Recreation

The Metropolitan Multi-Service Center provides opportunities for people with disabilities such as structured classes, a fitness room, full court gym, indoor heated pool, a beep baseball field, a tennis court, a quarter mile trail, and an urban garden. The possibilities are endless here! Just last year, a brand new, massive, colorful and accessible playground was built for the children. You can also participate in adaptive yoga, adult sports such as wheelchair basketball, rugby, soccer, tennis and power soccer. Come get fit at the MMSC in Houston!

Website: http://www.houstontx.gov/parks/adaptivesports.html
Phone: 713.284.1973

Handicap Van Rentals

If you're in the Greater Houston area and are in need of a handicap rental van, go visit Handicap Van Rentals! They are a family owned company that is open seven days a week to serve you. There are daily, weekly, monthly and even long term rental agreements that are reasonably priced.

Website: http://www.handicapvans.net
Phone: 713-723-8618
Email: doug10101@aol.com
Brain Injury Association of Texas- Support Group

Have you suffered a brain injury? Do you feel like no one can relate to what you've been through? The Brain Injury Association of Texas will help you find a support group with individuals who have similar experiences to you. Support groups can be found online on the BIATX website, which is very convenient. Find groups who are interested in outdoor activities and sports!

Facebook: http://www.facebook.com/pages/Brain-Injury-Association-of-Texas/115135759181
Phone: 512-326-1212

Email: info@biatx.org

Discovery Green

This non-profit park raises all funds for the activities and events that take place for Houstonians. Discovery Green ensures that it remains a fully accessible, incomparable public gathering place. There are several health and wellness activities, special events such as a monthly vintage market, entertainment, art, trails, boat rentals, and more! There is always something going on, even on the weekends, so come join in on the fun!

Website: http://www.discoverygreen.com/
Facebook: http://www.facebook.com/DiscoveryGreenHouston
Phone: 713-400-7336

Eels On Wheels

"The Eels on Wheels Adaptive Scuba Program is a registered 501(c)3 not-for-profit organization that provides people the opportunity to dive at their own ability level by certifying divers through the Handicapped Scuba Association (HSA)."

Website: http://www.eels.org/
Facebook: https://www.facebook.com/groups/eelsonwheels/
Email: eelsonwheels@sbcglobal.net

Wheelchair Accessible Wildlife Viewing Sites in Texas

This is a resource full of wildlife viewing sites in Texas that are wheelchair-accessible. This list is offered as a public service, offering a variety of accessible trails, historic sites, wildlife management areas, education centers, community parks and more.

Website: http://tpwd.texas.gov/landwater/land/programs/tourism/wheelchair_access/
Email: NatureTourism@tpwd.state.tx.us.
Facebook: https://www.facebook.com/texasparksandwildlife

Texas Adaptive Aquatics

"TEXAS ADAPTIVE AQUATICS (T.A.A.) features an outstanding adaptive water skiing program that allows people with physical and/or mental disabilities the opportunity to discover the thrill and excitement of water skiing, sailing, and kayaking. T.A.A. founded in 1989 and incorporated in the State of Texas in 1990, is a non-profit sports training program for children and adults with disabilities."

Website: http://taasports.org/index.php
Phone: (281) 324-4653
Facebook: https://www.facebook.com/texasadaptiveaquatics?ref=ts

National Veterans Wheelchair Games

"Co-Presented by the Department of Veterans Affairs and the Paralyzed Veterans of America, the National Veterans Wheelchair Games is a rehabilitation and wheelchair sports program empowering Veterans with spinal cord injuries, multiple sclerosis, amputations and other neurological injuries to live more active and healthy lives through wheelchair sports and recreation."

"Each summer, Veterans from across the United States, including a team from Great Britain, travel to a new community hosting the NVWG. During the week, Veterans compete in 18 wheelchair sports events while providing encouragement and mentoring for new Veterans."

Website: http://wheelchairgames.org/
Email: tombrown@pva.org
Facebook: https://www.facebook.com/wheelchairgames

Utah

"Whether you come to ski or snowboard "The Greatest Snow on Earth," to mountain bike Slickrock in Moab Utah, to take a summer whitewater rafting splash down Cataract Canyon, or to visit the Old West with a tour of outlaw hideouts and stickups, Utah has adventure waiting." (source: http://www.utah.com/)

Utah Accessible Travel Guide

The Utah Office of Tourism has launched a new guide to Accessible Utah, featuring a range of resources available to disabled travelers, including airport and car rental facilities, American Disability Act (ADA) campsites and trails, and a selection of activities and attractions. The guide will take you to the state's accessible national and state parks, prime attractions in the area, and local non-profit organizations specializing in adaptive recreation adventures. Get yours at: http://www.visitutah.com/plan-your-trip/accessible-utah

Splore

This Utah non-profit organization is known for starting the first accessible rafting program in the state, and specializes in creating empowering experiences through affordable, customized recreation and education programs for people of all abilities.

Phone: 801-484-4128
Website: www.splore.org
Facebook: http://www.facebook.com/gosplore

The Kostopulos Dream Foundation

This foundation is dedicated to improving the lives of people with disabilities through recreation and leisure education.

Phone: 801-582-0700
Website: www.campk.org

Wasatch Adaptive Sports

This sporting program specializes in winter programs such as skiing, snowshoeing and sled hockey.

Phone: 801-933-2188
Website: www.wasatchadaptivesports.org

Vermont

"From a romantic weekend getaway to a vacation at a family resort, a trip to New England takes you to a distinctly American region rich in history, culture, and natural beauty." (Source: VisitNewEngland.com)

Vermont Adaptive

"Vermont Adaptive Ski and Sports is the largest year-round disabled sports non-profit organization in Vermont offering the most diverse program opportunities and unique, specialized equipment. Vermont Adaptive promotes independence and furthers equality through access and instruction to sports and recreational opportunities including alpine skiing, snowboarding, and other winter sports; kayaking, canoeing, sailing, cycling, hiking, rock climbing, tennis, horseback riding, and more. We serve clients of all abilities with physical, cognitive and emotional disabilities from all over the world in three locations in Vermont during the winter – Killington Resort and Pico Mountain in Killington; Sugarbush Resort in Warren; and Bolton Valley in Bolton. Summer programs are provided state-wide."

Website: www.vermontadaptive.org
Phone: 802.786.4991
Facebook: http://www.facebook.com/pages/Vermont-Adaptive-Ski-Sports/91655724291

AbilityPlus Adaptive Sports

"AbilityPLUS adaptive sports programs are tailored to the needs of participating individuals. Staff and volunteers have backgrounds in education, special education, physical and occupational therapy as well as the legal and medical fields. Volunteers from all backgrounds receive extensive training and participate in ongoing workshops to keep them current on the most recent adaptive techniques and specialized equipment."

Program activities include but are not limited to:
- ALPINE SKIING
- CROSS-COUNTRY SKIING
- SNOWBOARDING
- SNOWSHOEING
- KAYAKING
- EQUESTRIAN
- CYCLING
- GOLF
- HIKING
- WATERSKIING
- SWIMMING

Website: www.abilityplus.org
Email: info@abilityplus.org
Phone: 800.287.8415
Facebook: http://www.facebook.com/AbilityPlusAdaptive

Virginia

"What you'll love about Virginia is its devotion to the stories, experiences and people who make us what we are today. Wherever you find yourself - in a garden, at an art museum, performance hall or theme park - you might discover something that sparks a life-long interest." (source: http://www.virginia.org/)

USTA Adaptive Tennis Virginia

The USTA Adaptive Tennis mission is to provide opportunities to everyone, regardless of any disability, to enjoy tennis. Adaptive Tennis' goal is to promote and develop recreational tennis opportunities for individuals with differing abilities and circumstances through inclusion, knowledge, and support, and by providing, where needed, adaptive programming, equipment, and teaching techniques.

Website: http://www.usta.com/Adult-Tennis/Adaptive-Tennis/Information/usta_adaptive_tennis_registered_programs/
Facebook: https://www.facebook.com/USTA
Phone: 540-982-5524

SportAble Adaptive Sports & Recreation

The reason Sportable exists is to transform the lives of people with physical and visual disabilities through sport! Offers several sports including but not limited to: strength training, cycling, tennis and archery.

Website: http://sportable.org/
Facebook: http://www.facebook.com/SportableRVA
Phone: 804.340.2991

Wintergreen Adaptive Sports

Wintergreen Adaptive Sports is a non-profit, 501(c)3 corporation whose mission is to improve the lives of people with a disability through outdoor sports and recreation. As of 2010, we offer instruction in alpine skiing, snowboarding, kayaking, and canoeing. In addition, in 2009 we created our first Wounded Warrior golf program. Located in the Blue Ridge Mountains of Virginia, next to the slopes of Wintergreen Resort and adjacent to Wintergreen's beautiful Lake Monocan, WAS offers fun, exhilaration and the opportunity to enjoy the outdoors with family and friends.

Website: http://skiwas.org/
Facebook: http://www.facebook.com/pages/Wintergreen-Adaptive-Sports/196084620405507
Phone: 434-325-2007

Accessible Virginia

"Accessible Virginia gives extraordinarily detailed descriptions of Virginia attractions, lodging, bed and breakfasts, restaurants, outdoor recreation and shopping facilities that meet the needs of travelers of varied abilities. This web site provides comprehensive information such as locations and measurements of doors, aisles, stairways and bathroom facilities, as well as listings of dialysis centers, equipment repair locations and even veterinarians for assistance animals."

Website: http://www.accessiblevirginia.org/
Email: contactus@accessiblevirginia.org
Facebook: https://www.facebook.com/pages/Accessible-Virginia/95944367917?v=wall

Accessible Fishing

The Virginia Department of Game and Inland Fisheries provide a list of accessible fishing spots for people with disabilities.

Website: http://www.dgif.virginia.gov/fishing/accessible/index.asp?waterbody=&location=all
Email: dgifweb@dgif.virginia.gov
Facebook: https://www.facebook.com/VDGIF

Patty Kunze is a big fan of Colonial Williamsburg in Virginia. The uniformed fifer is her son. She enjoys all of his historical reenactment marches. Photo courtesy of Get Out & Enjoy Life Campaign.

Washington

"Washington State is known for its lattes, software companies and its music scene. You can also retrace the lives of beloved Twilight characters on the Olympic Peninsula, sip award-winning wines and take a trip up in the iconic Space Needle.

From the open skies of Eastern Washington's high desert country, across the abundant valleys of our rich agricultural regions, to the wild Pacific Ocean beaches, it's no wonder that Washington - the State - is often compared to the song, "America, the Beautiful." And all of this is within easy reach from our vibrant urban centers and communities, teeming with fine dining and cultural happenings all year long. In Washington, you can enjoy several vacations in one. Or come back for new discoveries." (source: http://www.experiencewa.com/)

Bill Bokesz sees the sights in Seattle, on his way to an Alaskan cruise! Picture courtesy of Get Out, Enjoy Life campaign.

Community Integration Program

"Community Integration Services provides aquatic experiences for people of all ages who have special developmental or physical needs. We help our clients to access community pool facilities for recreation, rehabilitation, swimming and general fitness. Through adaptive equipment, personalized instructions, and the healing powers of the water, our clients experience greater independence and enjoyment of life."

Website: http://www.cisaquatics.com/index.html
Phone: (425) 830-7746
Email: harrietott@comcast.net

Outdoors for All

"The Outdoors for All Foundation is a national leader and one of the largest nonprofit organizations providing year round instruction in outdoor recreation for people with physical, developmental, and sensory disabilities since 1978."

Website: http://www.outdoorsforall.org
Phone: 206.838.6030
Email: info@outdoorsforall.org

iFly Seattle

"Come and experience indoor skydiving at iFLY Seattle. It is safe for kids, challenging for adults, exciting for teens and realistic for skydivers. No experience necessary and it is great fun for all ages, three and up!"

Website: www.iflyseattle.com
Phone: (206) 244-iFLY
Email: nfo@iFLYseattle.com
Facebook: https://www.facebook.com/iFlyFanPage?ref=hl

Seattle Adaptive Sports

"Seattle Adaptive Sports is a not-for-profit organization, tax-exempt under section 501(c)(3) of the Internal Revenue Code. SAS is dedicated to the promotion of the well being of physically challenged individuals, by giving them the opportunity to participate and compete in athletic and recreational activities, including basketball and track. SAS participants benefit from the physical activity and socialization opportunities offered by the organization, improving self-esteem and physical well being, as well as independence.

SAS serves over 100 athletes from the Western Washington area, as well as sponsoring events drawing teams from across the country. Our athletes are physically challenged with disabilities including amputation, spinal cord injuries, cerebral palsy, low vision, joint damage, severe scoliosis, spina bifida, transverse myelitis, trauma brain injury, and other congenital or acquired conditions affecting their mobility."

Website: http://www.seattleadaptivesports.org/
Phone: 206.726.3984
Email: info@seattleadaptivesports.org
Facebook: http://www.facebook.com/seattleadaptivesports

National Museum of Natural History

"The National Museum of Natural History (NMNH) is part of the Smithsonian Institution, the world's preeminent museum and research complex. The Museum is dedicated to inspiring curiosity, discovery, and learning about the natural world through its unparalleled research, collections, exhibitions, and education outreach programs. Opened in 1910, the green-domed museum on the National Mall was among the first Smithsonian building constructed exclusively to house the national collections and research facilities."

Website: http://www.mnh.si.edu/visit/accessibility.htm
Email: naturalexperience@si.edu
Facebook: https://www.facebook.com/nmnh.fanpage

Accessing Washington Outdoors

"Washington State is recognized for its wide array of outdoor recreational activities and wildlife. The Department of Fish and Wildlife (WDFW) encourages all persons with a disability to experience recreation in Washington's wonderful outdoors. Numerous opportunities are offered for hunters and anglers with disabilities through legislative mandates, statues, and policies complying with provisions of the Americans with Disabilities Act (ADA)."

Website: http://wdfw.wa.gov/accessibility/
Facebook: https://www.facebook.com/WashingtonFishWildlife

Washington, DC

"Visit Washington, DC and stand on the steps of the Lincoln Memorial, walk the halls of the White House and the U.S. Capitol, and tour the free exhibits of the Smithsonian museums. Whether you're coming to town for the Cherry Blossom Festival or to tour the monuments and memorials, this is a trip that will be enjoyed by the whole family. (source: http://thedistrict.com/)

The Metro – Accessibility

All Metro stations and rail cars are accessible. There are several handicapped parking places, extra-wide ramps and faregates and elevators. Rail cars feature gap reducers between the car and the platform. To find out more information, please visit their website. There is also information about obtaining a Metro Disability ID Card, extra accessibility information and more!
Website: http://www.wmata.com/accessibility/
Phone: 202-637-7000

Megan Hammond in Washington DC at the first inaugural Roll on Capitol Hill in 2012. Picture courtesy of the Get Out, Enjoy Life campaign.

The Metro Buses – Accessibility

The Washington D.C. Metro Buses are fully accessible and convenient to use while traveling throughout the city. All buses kneel or lower to make entrances and exits easier and quicker. There is priority seating for those with disabilities as well as wheelchair ramps or lifts. If the hydraulic lift system malfunctions, it can be operated manually for 100% reliability. Each bus contains two wheelchair securement areas in the front and includes tie-down and lap belts for safety. There is an accessible yellow button next to the wheelchair securement area so the customer can alert the driver of his or her next stop.
Website: http://www.wmata.com/accessibility/metrobus.cfm

Phone: 202-637-7000

MetroAccess Paratransit

This is a shared ride, door to door paratransit service for people who do not want to use the bus or metro. The MetroAccess Paratransit is a quick, easy and efficient way to book trips throughout the WashingtonD.C.metropolitan region. Please visit their website to check out prices, hours of operation and more!

Website: http://www.wmata.com/accessibility/metroaccess_service/
Phone: 202-637-7000

MedStar National Rehabilitation Network -Wheelchair Basketball

MedStar NRH offers free wheelchair basketball clinics on Wednesdays from 6:00 p.m. until 8:00 p.m. at the Emory Recreation Center. All ages and disabilities are welcome to come learn the basics of this exciting sport!

Website: http://www.nrhrehab.org/Patient+Care/Sports+Programs/Wheelchair+Basketball/default.aspx
Facebook: https://www.facebook.com/MedStarNRH?fref=ts
Phone: 202.877.1441

MedStar National Rehabilitation Network – Quad Rugby

MedStar NRH offers free quad rugby clinics on Thursdays from 6:00 p.m. – 8:30 p.m. at the King Green leaf Recreation Center. The team has recently joined the United States Quad Rugby Association and has recently attended tournaments in Pennsylvania!

Video: http://www.youtube.com/watch?v=NMvDyaT9hC8&feature=player_embedded
Website: http://www.nrhrehab.org/Patient+Care/Sports+Programs/Quad+Rugby/default.aspx
Phone: 202.877.1417

Wisconsin

"Wisconsin boasts some amazing vacation destinations that feature a wide range of activities all set against the beautiful backdrop we call the Badger State.

Whether you enjoy outdoor activities like hiking, biking, fishing or kayaking, or those indoors like shopping, museums and art galleries you won't be disappointed." (source: http://www.escapetowisconsin.com/)

Adaptive Sportsmen

Adaptive Sportsmen's mission is to provide recreational activities and opportunities for people with disabilities. Members are able to hunt, fish, boat, do archery and more. There are even fishing piers and waterfowl blinds that are fully accessible.

Website: http://adaptivesportsmen.org/
Phone: 262-378-2092
Email: aneu@adaptivesportsman.org

North American Squirrel Association (NASA) – Outdoor Fun For Seniors and the Physically Challenged

NASA is a non-profit organization that strives to provide senior citizens and people with disabilities with the ability to hunt and fish. With donated funds and equipment, several citizens have joined in on the fun for no cost! NASA also offers fun outdoor activities such as adaptive skiing, golf, and bicycling.

Website: http://www.nasasquirrel.org/
Phone: 608-234-5988

Milwaukee Recreation

Milwaukee Recreation's Therapeutic Recreation program offers programs for people with disabilities over the age of three. There is a wide variety of activities and events to choose from, anywhere from swimming to scrapbooking. The opportunities are endless. Milwaukee Recreation wants to ensure that camp members gain meaningful relationships and trust along with amazing experiences in activities.

Website: http://www.milwaukeerecreation.net/therapeutic/
Phone: 414- 647-6065

VSA Wisconsin -The State Organization On Arts and Disability

This organization believes in celebrating the accomplishments of children and adults with disabilities through dance, drama, creative writing, music and visual art throughout Wisconsin. The goal is to provide an outlet of creativity and endless possibilities for personal, academic and professional success. Talents of people with disabilities are showcased through performances, exhibitions and special events.

Website: http://www.vsawis.org/
Facebook: http://www.facebook.com/pages/VSA-Wisconsin/177473065073
Phone: 608-241-2131

Wisconsin Badger Camp

The mission is to provide quality outdoor recreational experiences for people with disabilities. People will fully understand their surroundings and meet their full potential at the Wisconsin Badger Camp. Campers will gain social skills, independence and meaningful relationships. All disabilities are welcome here—down syndrome, cerebral palsy or people in wheelchairs.

Website: http://www.badgercamp.org/
Facebook: http://www.facebook.com/pages/Wisconsin-Badger-Camp/129459937097069
Phone: 608-348-9689

Fishing Has No Boundaries

"Fishing Has No Boundaries®, Inc. (FHNB) is a non-profit 501-C3 organization whose goal is to open up the great outdoors for people with disabilities through the world of fishing. FHNB has grown into a National Organization with 27 chapters in 13 states, enabling thousands of individuals with disabilities to participate fully in this spirit lifting, morale booster, trouble free recreational activity. Continue to look for additional announcements for new chapters in new states, opening up new dreams for persons with disabilities that might not otherwise experience what you or I might just take for granted."

Website: http://www.fhnbinc.org/
Phone: 800-243-3462
Facebook: https://www.facebook.com/FHNBInc

Wheelchair Basketball Camp

"Athletes planning on attending this camp should be extremely independent and have a strong interest in competitive basketball. Athletes will participate in a variety of stations focusing on both individual and team concepts, and will be instructed by some of the best wheelchair basketball players in the world."

"This camp will offer the participant/athlete opportunities to grow physically, mentally, and emotionally through participation in a variety of sporting activities and through instruction with peers and camp staff."

Website: http://www.uww.edu/ce/camps/athletic/basketball/wheelchairbball
Email: cesevents@uww.edu
Facebook: https://www.facebook.com/WarhawkWheelchairBasketballCamp

Wyoming

"Wyoming is a place of unspoiled mountain vistas and vast forested wilderness. It's also home of Yellowstone and Grand Teton National Parks. This state is one of the few remaining parts of the United States where the

West is indeed still wild. Stay at an authentic dude ranch, soak in hot springs, experience the thrill of a rodeo or fish in the crystal-clear streams." (source: http://www.discoveramerica.com/usa/states/wyoming.aspx)

Teton Adaptive Sports

"Teton Adaptive Sports (TAS) was formed in the spring of 2005 in Teton County and is the first non-profit in Wyoming to be associated as a chapter with Disabled Sports/USA. Our mission is to promote and support sports and recreation opportunities for people with disabilities living in and visiting the Greater Teton Area. Headquartered in Jackson Hole, Teton Adaptive Sports is centered in a region known for endless outdoor adventures. "

Website: http://tetonadaptivesports.com/
Phone: 307 699 3554
Email: info@adaptivesports.com

Yellowstone National Park

"Many facilities are more than a century old and accessibility is not always ideal. However, we are improving accessibility as quickly as possible within funding limitations. Facilities described as accessible do not necessarily comply fully with federal standards. Some accessible facilities are not marked with the international symbol."

Website: http://www.nps.gov/yell/planyourvisit/accessibility.htm
Accessible Guide (PDF):
http://www.nps.gov/yell/planyourvisit/loader.cfm?csModule=security/getfile&PageID=496175

Footloose Sailing Association

"Footloose is a 100% volunteer summer sailing program for the disabled that features events including day sailing and a weekend cruise across Puget Sound to spend the night camping on Blake Island. In the winter, the organization holds several social activities including a potluck, fundraising and training sessions."

Website: http://www.footloosedisabledsailing.org/
Phone: 206-382-2680
Facebook: https://www.facebook.com/FootlooseSailingAssociation

Additional Travel Sources

California resident Julie Jones storms the Tower Bridge in London, England! Picture courtesy of Get Out, Enjoy Life campaign.

Access-Able Travel Source

"We have information and resources about:
- Travel with a special need.
- Disability magazines.
- Access guides for cities, resorts and attractions.
- Wheelchair or scooter rentals.
- Accessible transportation and more

Website: http://access-able.com/graphical_index.html
Email: information@access-able.com

Accessible Journeys

"Accessible Journeys is a vacation planner and tour operator exclusively for wheelchair travelers, their families and friends. Since 1985, wheelchair accessible vacation travel has been our only job."

Our accessible lifestyle vacations are for slow walkers, wheelchair travelers, their families and their friends. Our travel services include:

- Accessible vacation planning
- Accessible Group Tours
- Accessible Group Cruises
- Individual Accessible Cruises
- Licensed Travel Companions
- Disability Travel Resources

Website: http://www.disabilitytravel.com/
Phone: 800-846-4537

Wilderness Inquiry

"We are a non-profit adventure travel organization on a mission of connecting everyone to great places through activities such as sea kayaking, canoeing, rafting, hiking, safaris and dogsledding. Our adventures take you all over the world, from the Mississippi River to East Africa on high quality experiences featuring carefully crafted itineraries, excellent food, top notch gear and, best of all, highly skilled trail guides who care deeply about providing you the very best experience possible."

"Wilderness Inquiry is all about access, inclusion, and opportunity. We believe exploration of the natural world is a birthright we all share, and we act on that belief. We operate in a manner that facilitates full participation by everyone, including people of all backgrounds, ages, and abilities."

Website: https://www.wildernessinquiry.org/about-wilderness-inquiry/is-wilderness-inquiry-for-you/integrated-adventures-for-persons-with-disabilities/
Email: info@wildernessinquiry.org
Facebook: https://www.facebook.com/WildernessInquiry

Israel for All

"Interested in a tour of a lifetime? Like to visit the most impressive well known places you heard about and never went to? Do you like to relay on our experience handling your needs and abilities? Our experienced tour guides are waiting to show you the Holy Land. Come with us and engage the land of Israel, meet Israelis in a way you didn't do before."

Website: http://www.israel4all.com/tour/upcoming-open-tours-2/
Facebook: https://www.facebook.com/Israel4All

Access 2 Africa Safaris

"Safaris and tours for all travelers including families with children, individuals, groups and honeymooners. We specialize in wheelchair friendly and accessible tours, safaris and travel for the disabled, handicapped and mobility impaired including deaf(hearing impaired) and blind(visually impaired) guests."

Website: http://www.access2africasafaris.com/
Email: info@access2africasafaris.co.za
Facebook: https://www.facebook.com/pages/Access2africa-Safaris/122813524399833

Gimp On The Go

"We're very proud to host the web's most comprehensive list of disability-friendly ground transportation and tour operators for the most common ports of call for both sea cruises and river cruises world-wide! Check it out in Travel Resources! Let us know if you have any additions."

Website: http://www.gimponthego.com/#

Curb Free with Cory Lee

Curb Free with Cory Lee is a wheelchair accessible travel guide to destinations around the globe. Here, Wheelchair user Cory Lee, shares his experiences in traveling, what locations are accessible, and how to make the right preparations before booking a flight.

Website: http://www.curbfreewithcorylee.com/
Facebook: https://www.facebook.com/CurbFree?fref=ts

Disabled Accessible Travel

"Arriving at an airport after a long flight, short haul or international, and having to find wheelchair accessible transport to get you to your hotel (reservation service available) can be a stressful business. In Barcelona, Girona & Reus we take that stress away by providing you with transfers in 100% wheelchair and scooter accessible vehicles fitted with all the latest safety features. Our drivers speak a variety of languages and provide a personal service that includes waiting for you in the Arrivals area (no searching for your transport required!), assisting with baggage, and answering any questions you might have. An optional extra special service we provide is a 'meet & greet' by one of our representatives who will take care of all your needs from airport to your hotel reception desk."

Website: http://www.disabledaccessibletravel.com/business.html
Facebook: https://www.facebook.com/disabledaccessibletravel

Castillo San Cristóbal

"Accessible parking is available at the main entrance of the park (on Calle Muñoz-Rivera). Within the main entrance area (former Civil Defense Building) there are accessible restrooms, water fountains, a bookstore and a theater. From this entrance an elevator provides access to the main plaza or the first floor of the fort. The upper levels are accessible via steep, historic ramps.

The historic entrance on Calle Norzagaray is also accessible, but up a steep ramp. There are accessible restrooms and water fountains throughout the main plaza level. The tunnel leading to the dungeon is considered "accessible" but the tunnel leading back to the main entrance area is not."

Website: http://www.nps.gov/saju/planyourvisit/accessibility.htm
Phone: 787-729-6960

San Juan Trolley System

San Juan has a trolley system in place, and some of the trolleys are wheelchair accessible. It is worth noting that these "trolleys" are actually just buses painted to look like trolleys. The system has stops located all over Old San Juan and near the forts, most of which are wheelchair accessible. There are two different routes one can take, depending on the desired destination. Trolley stop (terminal one) is located across the street from cruise ship terminal 4. The trolley is free and people are able to get on and off at marked trolley stops. Since San Juan is a city full of hills and cobble stones streets, taking the trolley makes it convenient to get to a destination. Also, Old San Juan can get extremely hot! Most of the trolley cars are equipped with air-conditioning, but a few are open air trolleys.

National Parks and Golden Access Pass

National and state parks abound and many offer a broad range of accessible including campgrounds, fishing spots, trails and picnic areas. For travelers with disabilities, the Golden Access Passport is free and gives users free entry to all national parks, plus 50% off fees for the uses of many park facilities and services. To get a Golden Access pass, you must show proof of age, US citizenship or permanent residency and proof of disability. You can request your Golden Access Pass by mail or by internet.

To order passes by mail:

National Park Service
1849 C Street NW
Washington DC 20240
202-208-4747

To order online, visit www.nps.gov

Share Your Own Story of Discovering

Thank you for reading Wheel:Life's third book, *Discovering: Accessible US Travel Guide for Wheelchair Users*. We hope that some of the destinations we have shared in the previous chapters have inspired you with new ways you can connect with friends, family and the community around you.

The $1.99 that you paid for this book is earmarked to fund additional Wheel:Life programs so that we can continue to provide support and resources to the wheelchair community that we serve, worldwide!

However, we realize that if you are reading this book, you may also have a personal story or favorite vacation spot of your own that could help other people who also use wheelchairs.

If you'd like to share your own story about a travel experience to help encourage others, please email the Wheel:Life team at info@wheel-life.org.

If we choose your personal anecdote as an example to use within the next book in this series, we'll send you $100 that can go toward purchasing your own equipment, medical supplies or medical care. Yes, it's that simple!

So get those ideas down on paper, we're excited to hear about the amazing and unique ways that you have helped yourself or a friend/family member who has a disability.

Thank you again for being part of Wheel:Life! We hope you'll visit our main website at www.wheel-life.org to stay connected and take part in the ongoing free resources that we share daily on the site.

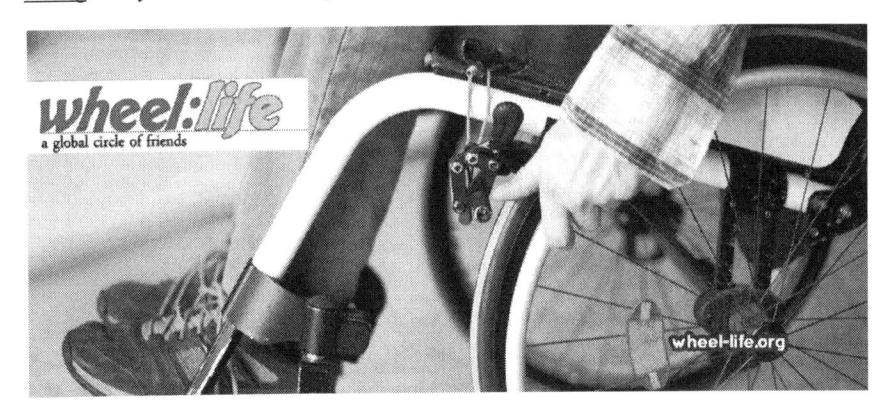

Dedication

This book is dedicated to someone who was instrumental in creating the annual Get Out & Enjoy Life accessible travel program from the ground up, without which this book would have never been written. He has worked tirelessly [and sometimes not so], contributing his time and efforts to build an ongoing resource to help friends who use wheelchairs in exploring their world.

Christopher DiVirgilio, Digital Editor of SPORTS 'N SPOKES magazine and PN magazine – thank you from the bottom of my heart! I am honored to be your friend and peer in serving the wheelchair community. Thank you for recognizing the potential in this program more than five years ago.

Time flies when you're having fun. Chris, you make our world so much more fun just by being part of it. Your humble commitment to lifting up your fellow Veterans is unmatched. Countless numbers of wheelchair users who benefit from your daily work would be at such a loss without your kind, unwavering support and encouragement.

Like my own journey, your path to helping others was guided by a friend who introduced you years ago to the challenges of using a wheelchair. I am so thankful that he set you on this path as it led to us become friends and lifelong advocates. We are incredibly blessed.

Proverbs 2:1-9   *Join us at www.wheel-life.org.*

Wheel:Life Book Series

If you enjoyed this book, then you'll love these other books from Wheel:Life.

10 Fundraising Ideas to Help People with Disabilities

In this book, you'll review 10 brainstorming ideas for different types of fundraiser events to benefit an individual with a disability who needs assistance for medical equipment, physical rehabilitation, adaptive sports equipment or daily medical needs. Throughout the book, Lisa Wells shares real-life examples and success stories from her interactions with disability advocates, non-profit supporters and Wheel:Life members throughout a healthcare marketing career that spans more than 20 years on three continents.

10 Fundraising Ideas to Help People with Disabilities features interviews from:

- Paralympian and UroMed founder Bert Burns on how he raised support to begin his career in wheelchair racing
- Project Walk Atlanta participant Leslie Ostrander on how she raised money for additional rehab
- The founders of 100 Songs for Kids on their annual music event to benefit children's medical charities
- Rolling Inspiration creator Chris Salas on how he lined up sponsors for his SCI peer support group and power soccer team
- The creators of Hunter's Torch Daylily Garden, a fundraising resource for a child with special needs.
- The Independence Fund - a little known source of financial support for disabled US veterans.

If you have a disability, and a facing a financial challenge, you can request a free copy of this book at: www.wheel-life.org/free-book-series.

Or, to purchase this book through Amazon, go to http://amzn.to/1UuAhMo

Reconnecting: Relationship Advice from Wheelchair Users

In this book, you'll hear from six people who use wheelchairs as they share their perspective on friends, family and relationships including dating, marriage and parenting. Throughout the book, Lisa Wells shares real-life examples and success stories from her interactions with disability advocates, non-profit supporters and Wheel:Life members throughout a healthcare marketing career that spans more than 20 years on three continents.

Reconnecting features interviews from:

- Graduate student & quadriplegic Ather Sharif about connecting on a college campus
- Quadriplegic Eric Kolar on connecting with friends through car audio competitions
- Amputee Thomas Morris on connecting through his unique appearance and personality
- NSCIA Buffalo NY President Natalie Barnhard who connects Wheels with Wings
- Paraplegic Todd Robinson who explains his family connection through the joy of adoption
- Quadriplegic Ashleigh Justice who connects on the quad rugby field and as a young mother

If you have a disability, and a facing a financial challenge, you can request a free copy of this book at: http://wheel-life.org/free-book-series/

Or, to purchase this book through Amazon, go to http://amzn.to/1CjpiPW

Made in the USA
Middletown, DE
23 May 2017